20th Century Garden and Landscape Architecture in the Netherlands

Gerritjan Deunk

20th Century Garden and Landscape Architecture in the Netherlands

NAi Publishers

Rotterdam

Contents

Preface

Garden and landscape architecture of the twentieth century is a non-concept. Architects build and their final aim is a real house or building, after which there will not be any significant changes for a fair length of time, or so we hope in most cases. Fashion, decay or other architects would be necessary to change the existing construction. Results produced by garden and landscape architects, on the other hand, rather resemble a perpetuum mobile. When it is delivered, the result of the design envisaged is not there yet and the optimal form has not yet reached its full growth. How does one capture a garden or a park, when does one judge its form, constantly in motion through the decades and subject to the whims of man and nature? Which architect provided the final design and at what time? And, was it really his realm of ideas or were they borrowed thoughts? What will be left of the original design for a park, once the first generation of trees has fallen down and two generations of council architects and Parks and Public Gardens Departments have left an abundance of marks, or too few marks?

Plenty. Enough, at least, to enable us to give a summary, incomplete, very visual survey of the development of green areas in the Netherlands from the beginning of the twentieth century. Then, the distinction between landscape and garden was still very much in evidence: a distinction between savage and cultivated land. Designers mostly determine the landscape as far as it falls within the boundaries of a country estate. The extensive developments of peat bogs and sandy areas produce landscapes that have been developed pragmatically, where water courses, soil conditions and the sizes of the parcels determine the shape. The reclamation of the Zuiderzee in the twentieth century marked the start of a period when 'new landscapes' had to be built continuously on a large scale. Agricultural specialists and landscape architects together had to find a form in which the new, carefully selected polder-residents can live and work contentedly and where, from the fifties on, they find recreational facilities. This development, from a traditional, closed landscape with polder farmers, to modern, open landscaped spaces is quite visible when one successively visits the reclaimed areas Wieringermeer, Noordoostpolder and Flevoland. The sequence of subsequent land consolidation projects also determined the evolving views on the Dutch landscape.

Round the year 2000 the concepts 'garden' and 'landscape' have become interchangeable. In the Netherlands, covered with buildings, it is hard to find an uninterrupted horizon. A visual axis focuses on a factory. Silence and darkness are at least as scarce as space. Designers can design private gardens and, at the same time, design rearrangements for country estates in one and the same practice. The planting or otherwise of sparse fields near airport runways or town squares without plants: it all comes under 'landscaping'. What are the limits for the concept 'landscaping'? Is the Haringvliet Dam landscape architecture?

The point of departure for this rough, and therefore subjective and debatable survey of 'green' culture in the past century, is to try and provide an insight into the broad outline of the development of gardens and landscapes to a wide, not learned circle of readers. 'Edutainment' in writing.

With the projects selected the name of the designer, a team of designers and as far as possible a school, views or interests are referred to in pictures and text. The result of the division in decades is that some periods are more interesting than others. It was not possible to mention all representatives of certain schools. Neither was it possible to highlight all sources of inspiration, precursors and circumstances. An attempt was made to follow the main line in design development and, besides, to show a few exceptions to the rule by means of quotations and subjects of discussion. Any selection does wrong to the non-included.

The periods garden and landscape architecture in this book have not been researched, discussed, crystallized and charted nearly as thoroughly as the corresponding periods in architecture. To the best of my knowledge there is no biography of Bijhouwer or the complete Mien Ruys book with a full survey of her works and her place in this special field. There is still plenty of scope for research and publications. Especially the reclamation of the Zuiderzee, the 'modern' years with a man like Hans Warnau, the part played by parks and gardens departments, still are largely virgin territory. Recording from oral reports would lead to flat contradictions. One person's hero is another's enemy. So, writing about it would be publishing without a safety net. In time the necessary corrections will have to be made. In twenty years from now this book should be written again.

   Legislation and plans have only been mentioned where they were essential to the clarity of the story. Notes have not been included. Quotations have been given mentioning the source. A bibliography is part of the book.

In my introduction I described the history of the statue garden of Kröller-Müller, since it can be said to be representative for the way nature was experienced in the Netherlands in the twentieth century.

   Per decade a plant breeder's catalogue has been added to give an impression of the development of selections and, besides, the way customers and products were approached. Here, Moerheim was chosen, because they were representative of plant breeders in that particular period, that happens to coincide with the scope of this book and, in addition, because of

the magnificent covers that reflect that period so well.

Writing a book is an exciting business. This voyage of discovery through the history of verdure is impossible without some indispensable guides from outside. I am indebted to the shadow readers on the critical professional panel: the encouraging Carla Oldenburger-Ebbers, the all-round Michael van Gessel, the modest Gaston Bekkers and the strict but fair Anne Mieke Backer. The latter's comments suffice to fill another book, let us say, in twenty years' time! Their honest 'phooey' in the margins kept me from many a beginner's mistake. Leo Kok read the manuscript as, in earlier days, he read my theses in the protestant secondary school in Aalten: devotedly, and with a keen sense of language. I also owe a debt of gratitude to Hans Ibelings who introduced me to the publisher, Simon Franke, who in turn guided me patiently, together with Paula Vaandrager, editor-in-chief Marianne Lahr and photo editor Ingrid Oosterheerd. Finally I wish to thank my valued colleague Lex Reitsma who again adds a carefully designed book to the already existing series.

Kröller-Müller

Kröller-Müller in the National Park De Hoge Veluwe
From Barren Wilderness to Culture in Nature

The history of gardens and landscaping in the twentieth century is clearly illustrated by the story of the national park De Hoge Veluwe and the statue garden that forms part of the Kröller-Müller Museum. Savage, and therefore useless land, was purchased by a wealthy couple at the beginning of the twentieth century for the purpose of serving as hunting grounds for the husband and the possibility of setting up a museum of fine arts in a suitable environment for the wife. The ultimate object is to donate the country estate ensemble to the nation, so that an unspoilt part of de Veluwe can be a sounding board for perception of nature and a preparation for enjoying sublime art: a borrowed and class conscious motive. The First World War and the stock exchange crash cause an interruption. In the course of the development process recreation becomes a new theme with totally different demands, wishes and motives. The museum of fine art is opened in 1939 and a few statues from the collection are put on show in the open. Lawns, rhododendrons and a tree-lined edge form the setting for abstract sculptures. During the seventies the woods were no longer adapted to the art, but the objects are fitted into the environment. Day trippers arrive, happily chattering on white bicycles. In the nineties the visual arts were almost invisible and apologetically present in the large pine wood. The difference between bronze artificial roots and the nearby tree is hardly visible. In the Museonder we see a bunch of roots from below and in the Landscapes Garden one gets an impression of the Veluwe during a half hour walk. Today, nature itself, with its peace and quiet has again become the centre of attention.

Savage land and honourable motives
'Between the drifting sands of the Central Veluwe and the southern edge of the Veluwe lies the national park De Hoge Veluwe, owned by the foundation bearing the same name', is a quote from the book Natuurmonumenten van Nederland [Preservation of Nature in the Netherlands] published in 1942. In 1926 a foundation was set up in order to bring this unique part of the Veluwe under a single management. It is a very varied landscape with many very different owners. Mr and Mrs Kröller-Müller are responsible for the major part of this area, which, amazingly, is not crossed by any public roads. The road from Otterlo to Hoenderloo was diverted for this purpose, entirely paid from private funds. The park is completely fenced in and there are four entrances. The main objective is hunting for him and founding a museum for her. For game stocks deer are imported from Poland. Since these have to fit inside square boxes, the new residents arrive with sawn-off antlers. Later mouflons are put out to make a home for themselves on the Veluwe. Apart from this large area other areas are acquired, bearing names such as the Black Mountain, the Otterlo Sands, the Pampelt and Hoog Barel. Another ten parcels of land follow. This gives an impression of the vastness of the whole area. This patchwork of plots eventually becomes one big park.

Thousands of hectares of natural and artificial forest
The drifting sands form an important part of De Hoge Veluwe; until the middle of the nineteenth century these were considered a threat to the wooded surroundings. To prevent expansion of the sand drifts so-called grooves were laid out; belts planted with pines, oaks and birches. In 1926 these belts were a characteristic, cultural element of the landscape. These avenues with

sometimes tall American oaks were seen as an unsuccessful, artificial element in a natural environment. The 'original type of forest is generally preferred'. For this reason the Natural Heritage Foundation contemplated an improvement of the forestland. For instance, the Scotch pine should be joined by the Corsican pine, the Japanese larch and the Douglas fir. In the deciduous forest Alpine mespilus, sweet chestnuts and hornbeams were to be added. The artificiality of the woods was emphasized by the statues that were placed in the park, including a statue of Christiaan de Wet by J.M. Mendes de Costa (1917), the memorial bench for the statesman Steyn created by Henry van de Velde and Antlers by John Rädeker (both around 1925). All this took place under the inspired direction of Mrs Kröller-Müller, who interfered in every small detail to do with landscaping. She wanted to see the result without labourers disturbing the picture. They should make themselves scarce behind the bushes and politely wait until madam had finished her tour of inspection. The total surface area of the park is 6,400 hectares, including 4,800 heather, drifting sands and savage space. Even then this was a unique situation in a densely populated country.

Hunting lodge with geraniums

In this natural environment some cultural settlements were built, such as the hunting lodge Sint Hubertus, designed by the architect H.P. Berlage in 1919. Again Natuurmonumenten van Nederland [Preservation of Nature in the Netherlands] criticized this as 'a far too pronounced building in this environment'. As a structure it is a unique Gesamtkunstwerk by Berlage, who not only created the building, but also decided on all details in the interior and produced the design for the formal gardens to the left and right of the main building. Bright red geraniums add colour to the walls and provide a bright horizontal element. In order to lend the building a good aura much of the surrounding area was adjusted. The drive round the pond provided arriving guests a long and wide view of the imposing building and the tower was reflected in the artificial pond with its asphalt bottom. The edge of the wood was enlivened with the planting of several exotic types of trees.

A great cultural heritage is given away

Comments in the above mentioned book on the big museum designed by the architect Henry van de Velde, that eventually was never built, were quite outspoken: 'A big chunk of red sandstone blocks on the highest, most visible spot in the park'. Now only a few foundations of the plans are visible. Lack of funds prevented their completion. A more modest set-up for a museum with a row of rooms round an indoor pond offered just enough space to accommodate the collection. It was opened in 1938. The collection and the entire park were donated to the Kingdom of the Netherlands and so became public property. Mr and Mrs Kröller-Müller enjoyed it for a short time only; they both died soon afterwards and were buried at their beloved De Hoge Veluwe. For many years to come the butler at the Hubertus Lodge would turn the pages of Mrs Müller's diary, containing personal poems and sayings.

Statues outside in a wooded garden

The small museum garden is the next step towards the statue garden that would later become famous. However, the book referred to earlier says: 'we feel more comfortable with the landscaping, or rather the landscape gardening set-up, in an environment of rhododendrons, under old pine trees, near the small pond, but in general this artistic beautification seems to be overdone'. Fifty years later we see that since then much has been 'beautified'. In 1960 the director of the museum, A.M. Hammacher wrote: 'In our time, when sculpture is developing in a new, unprecedented manner, a plan is being developed to enrich the park and the museum with a statue park, which will show this development in a concise and succinct manner.' In first instance the statue garden is a small garden with statues by, among others,

Lipschitz, Zadkine, Arp, Marini and Rodin. As early as 1954 J.T.P. Bijhouwer outlined the basis for the first part of the statue garden as we now know it: green spaces in the woods, where the art works can be viewed in peace and quiet against a decor of rhododendrons and pine trees. Meandering paths run along the manicured lawns and stretches of water. There we see a bright white, reflecting polyester sculpture by Marta Pan (1961), a hinged swan swaying and moving with the wind. In this garden we also find the pavilion designed by Gerrit Rietveld for the open-air exhibition in Sonsbeek. Half open and half closed spaces

show statues combined with green foliage, statues by Henry Moore and Barbara Hepworth, large round human shapes in dark bronze and white marble.

A view of woods and statues
The year 1977 marks a big change for the museum. The architect Wim Quist extended the old closed brick building by adding spacious, bright, austere rooms, with large glass walls commanding a splendid view of the nearby nature. The entrance was under the trees, inside the museum a neon sculpture winked at the visitors. One wall of the corridor was a closed wall, the other one large window offer-ing a view of woods, pine cones and foxglove. One could almost touch it, but still one was safe behind the glass. Even when one had a sandwich on the museum terrace of Monsieur Jacques' restaurant, the shining blue lamps of Dan Flavin or the white garden furniture of Fortuyn/O'Brien between the foliage attracted the attention. Just as well, according to the critic Lucette ter Borg in her column 'Museum Food' in the daily de Volkskrant, thirty years later. The very contemporary art is miles ahead of the 'snack bar food savoured in sunken sitting areas in the seventies.' Outside there was quite an evolution. Tall stacks of oil drums by Chris to broke through the old aesthetic limits. With their bright colours they are positioned in the middle of the meadow, between the crumbling wigwams by Cornelis van Rogge and wind vanes

by Ricky. The art is as temporary and vulnerable as nature itself. The visitor's imagination is clearly put to the test. In particular the Jardin d'email by Dubuffet, an enclosed space with black-edged white surfaces, of a repellent hostility in the middle of the verdure, provides a fresh view of the outside world. The perception of the artwork is compelling; it demands total submission. Entertainment value makes its entry.

Apologies to nature
In the eighties the intervention in nature became increasingly subtle. In his adoration of nature the artist Hamilton Finlay went to such lengths as to wrap trees in stone socles, so that they appear to stand on pedestals. On one of them the name Rousseau is displayed: back to nature. The ultimate apology to nature for the presence of culture was offered by the artist Penone. His bronze tree can hardly be distinguished from its surroundings. Its roots shine like those of its natural neighbour. Nature reflects the art. Rückriem's big stones, too, are closer to their environment than ever. From that moment on, the visitor stares vacantly into space. Anything in these woods can be art.

The statue garden all year round
With the extension carried out by Quist the museum underwent a complete change. The statue garden had slowly been expanded like a patchwork, following the successive fashions, but with little coherence. The statue garden was open to the public only during the summer, because the air conditioning system could not cope with dirty leaves and wet coats. The paths in the statue garden and the exhibited works were not totally winter hardy either. In 1995 Bureau West 8 was requested to present a plan for improvement. The various parts of the park and the museum were examined and their strong and weak points were noted. The entrance area to the museum was extended and more space was created for bicycles and statues near the entrance. In addition, air locks were installed at the entrance to the museum and the statue

garden. The paths were asphalted and on the old lawns in the Bijhouwer plan the sculptures were rearranged, classified in periods and zones. The Rietveld pavilion was renovated, the forest stand was cleaned up and rhododendrons were planted. Wherever possible, the promenade walk past the sculptures was more conveniently arranged. Gardeners were allowed to do their jobs in full view (Mrs Müller would have turned in her grave!), and visitors could again enjoy an uninhibited view of the hill and the statues were wrapped up against the cold. The sense of unity in park, garden and forest was reinforced.

Nature in ready-to-eat portions

11

The distinction between what is savage and civilized in De Hoge Veluwe is very neat. In a small surface area in the park protected by cattle grids, art is exhibited in a museum with a statue garden. Besides, for dozens of years visitors have been able to eat pancakes in a pastoral restaurant. In 1992 the Museonder was opened, a museum partly underground, where one can see from below how nature works. You can see that the ball of roots underground is bigger than the crown of the tree aboveground. Museum, shop and restaurant are arranged round a very orderly square with trees where many wooden benches stand in line, designed by the bureau of Bakker and Bleeker in 1985. A curiosity is the Landscapes Garden where you see various types of landscape from the Veluwe during a short walk and two heaps of sand where you can read about drifting sands, on a shiny silver plaque. Next to the Museonder there is the so-called park-shop, where the National Trust formula has been borrowed including the pencils with inscriptions. The shop, the museum, the Museonder, and the restaurant are conveniently arranged, close together. If you venture outside this cultural and educationally sound enclave on a sunny afternoon in June, you would usually be on your own. Near the Hubertus Lodge there is complete peace and quiet, except for the odd gunshot reports from soldiers exercising on the other side. In his solitude, General de

Wet looks over the fields, once intended to become the first statue garden by Mrs Kröller-Müller, and there is not a single cyclist around. The offspring of the Polish deer have all the space they need.

Getting a nice 'natural' feeling

In the fifties, mass tourism got its chance on the edge of the nature reserve. The time was not yet ripe, for a big swimming pond complete with coffee house near Otterlo remains empty due to lack of customers. Fifty years later this has been organized in a different and more concentrated manner. As a family you make a choice: you either go furniture-shopping, visit the town, give the dog a good run on the beach near Katwijk aan Zee or you decide to visit De Hoge Veluwe. Here, the supply and demand of nature are taken into account. If there is a greater demand for recreation on a sand drift, a sand project will be created, sponsored by an energy firm and a lottery. Right now, a big wish is a natural arena for big events. In this way the concept of experiencing nature is adjusted to the consumers' way of living every decade. It is easy to digest, for the coach drops you off on the doorstep of the visitors' centre of De Hoge Veluwe; or you have some exercise, take a white bicycle and cycle to the museum and the restaurant in about fifteen minutes. You can spend a few hours there, comfortable and indoors, you can buy a few things, walk around and enjoy a meal and you leave the park again in reverse order. And you will have that 'nice natural feeling'.

12

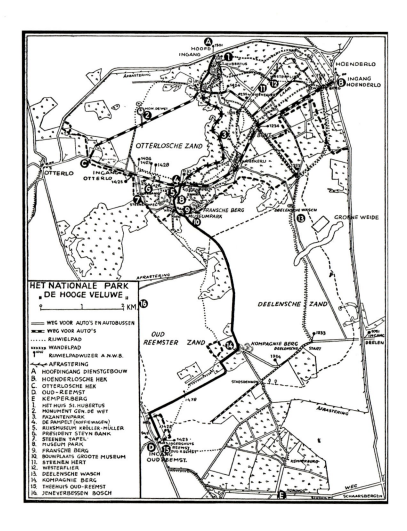

Educational sound arrangement of root ball of tree in the Museonder, National Park De Hoge Veluwe, Hoenderloo

National Park De Hoge Veluwe, Hoenderloo (1942)

Kröller-Müller Museum, Otterlo (situation 2001)

Bureau **West 8** is in the process of cleaning up the present stature park. It opens up spaces and arranges species of trees in groups. It highlights the French mountain again as a high point in the landscape. Besides, three footpaths are laid through the partly renovated statue garden of the Kröller-Müller Museum in Otterlo (1995-2002)

A picnic by car, within easy reach. National Park De Hoge Veluwe

J.T.P. Bijhouwer statue garden Kröller-Müller Museum, National Park De Hoge Veluwe (1955 and 1964)

1900-1910

• Belle époque up to 1914 • city parks and allotment gardens • a few designer families design many parks for country estates in the Netherlands • small gardens in residential areas and allotment gardens • architect designs gardens • broccoli and 'Zimmergurke'

Commuters, reclamation and protection
Like all of Western Europe, the Netherlands underwent profound and rapid changes around the year 1900. The country was not quite as crowded as a century later, but cities swelled due to industrialization and migration. Whereas in 1870 one in seven persons lived in a town, this figure had risen to one in four by 1925. New methods of transport affected people's way of life. Trains and trams allowed commuting over greater distances and cities in the western part of the country came within easy commuting distance from the Gooi region and the Utrecht hills. Factories relocated from the centre of towns to the outskirts or to the countryside, country estates were split up into residential areas and road and rail traffic intensified. New fertilizers made cultivation of poor sandy soils possible. Two companies, Heidemaatschappij and Grontmij (1915), were established to reclaim wastelands and, as importantly, to bring them under cultivation, which was a profitable business. The philosophy of these companies sharply contrasted with the ideas of Jacques P. Thijsse, an early nature conservationist who wished to preserve wastelands in their 'wild', natural state.

Conservation of nature, but what exactly is nature?
Interest in the outdoors grew. Due to urbanization and industrialization nature areas were valued more than previously and there was greater consideration for historical landscapes. Around the turn of the century several nature conservation societies were founded, including the Vereniging tot Bescherming van Vogels [Bird Protection Society], the Staatsbosbeheer [Forestry Commission] and the Vereniging tot Behoud van Natuurmonumenten [Society for the Preservation of Nature]. The latter, the Society for the Preservation of Nature, was founded by a small group of people who wished to prevent the City of Amsterdam from buying Lake Naardermeer and turning it into a rubbish dump. Instead, the society bought the lake itself. It did so in a very professional manner, setting a standard for the society's future success. Notaries and the bank Labouchère Oyens & Co., donating their services, provided the society with a sound legal and financial basis. By 1907 the Society for the Preservation of Nature had 872 members, mostly socially prominent persons. In those early days the society's office was simply a backroom in the home of its chairman, the lawyer P.G. van Tienhoven. To save money he delivered newsletters personally to members living nearby on the fashionable Herengracht and Keizergracht; the concept of overhead had not yet been invented at the time. From the outset the Society for the Preservation of Nature was convinced that its field of work should include not only nature areas but also country estates. The society received substantial revenue from production forests, which it used to finance its operation and to acquire more land. Receiving no government grants, financial independence ensured the society freedom of action. Jac. P. Thijsse wrote the text for a series of albums in which biscuit-buyers could paste the pictures of plant and animal life enclosed with Verkade's biscuits. As early as 1908 Thijsse advocated a landscape park to the south of Amsterdam. His Boschplan was a precursor of later plans leading to the present park, the Amsterdam Woods.

Preservation of nature, an international phenomenon

Social experiments like the Walden community, founded by the author/idealist Frederik van Eeden, also affected nature awareness – if only because van Eeden coined the phrase natuurmonument [nature reserve]. He rated the Beekbergerbos, thought to be the last remaining primeval forest in the Netherlands, as highly as 'ancient buildings for national art'. In the German language it is called Naturdenkmal, the French decided on Réserve biologique et artistique, while the Americans, already thinking in terms of recreation, described Yellowstone as a park 'for the benefit and the enjoyment of people'. These social thoughts were representative of the twentieth century's demand for more recreational facilities for more people with more spare time. On the other hand nature itself demanded more attention, being threatened from all sides. The nature versus culture, conflict versus harmony, conservation versus creation debate was to be a constant of the twentieth century.

Early city parks

For the first time in Dutch history there was demand for large-scale recreational facilities within cities. Around 1880 many large municipal parks were designed, many of which were indeed laid out. Names associated with this period are those of J.D. Zocher, Jr., L.P. Zocher (Vondelpark, Amsterdam), L.P. Roodbaart (Stadspark Leeuwarden, on the former city walls) and J.G. van Niftrik (Sarphatipark, Amsterdam). Everywhere town walls were torn down and promenades were made where the bourgeoisie could take their Sunday walk. It would take a long time and a lot of decision-making before a public park was finally realized. The Westbroekpark in The Hague is a case in point. For one thing there was the question whether the park was to be laid out in landscape style or architectural style, for another there were disputes between the garden architects and at least three municipal designers. L.P. Zocher submitted a first plan as

early as in 1880, and in 1922 Poortman made recommendations. It then took another seven years before the final modified plan was realized by Pieter Westbroek, an architect of the Municipal Parks and Public Gardens Department. A conflict of styles raged which was common in this period, landscape style or 'New Park' first, exclusive residential areas with gardens or a city park pur sang second. Modifications were implemented in the same year and later on in 1948 and 1994. The park will be mentioned further on for its National Perennials Garden and the famous rose garden in which exhibitions are held every year.

Allotments Committee

By the end of the nineteenth century the People's Association against Alcohol Abuse still gave out allotments to workers to keep them on the straight and narrow. Though small, the allotments allowed them to supplement their simple daily fare with fresh vegetables for the necessary vitamins. By 1909 the Allotments Committee developed a broader view; allotment gardens could also serve hard-working city-dwellers as a place to relax on the outskirts of the busy city. Land beside railway lines could be rented for a modest price, as it saved the railway companies the cost of maintenance. Allotments became private gardens for enthusiastic gardeners. During the world wars of the twentieth century the allotments proved to be especially useful for food production. At the beginning of the century the allotments were of an open character, the paths intersecting the gardens being open to the general public. All the same, the allotment holders developed a strong sense of community.

Cross-influences in country estate design

In the year 1853 Prince Frederik of the Netherlands engaged the garden architect C.E.A. Petzold to redesign palaces and country estates in The Hague and environs in late landscape style. On the country estates in particular, and especially in Wassenaar, Petzold added green belts and clusters of trees, as well as paths circling the park, to the existing meandering paths and group of trees. Friends of the royal family, such as the owners of the Weldam and Twickel estates, both situated in the province of Overijssel, followed in the wake of the House of Orange. Petzold was an authority on trees professionally, like his friend and colleague Leonard Springer. In 1924 they founded the Dutch Dendrological Society, which became an important meeting ground for landscape architects.

An influential architect of the early twentieth century was H.A.C. Poortman, a gifted designer who started out as an employee of Eduard André in Paris. His first project in the Netherlands was Weldam, where he restored the gardens on the basis of a plan made by his teacher. The assignment gave him plenty of scope to put his ideas about garden design into practice. After his work at Weldam, Poortman was asked to redesign other castle gardens, including an extensive rearrangement of the gardens of Middachten Castle (1900). Here he designed a formal garden in modern, regular style with a maze, a parterre de broderie (an ornamental bed with boxwood flower and leaf motifs alternating with filling materials like shells and broken stones), a rose garden, a croquet field and a boulingrin (a sunken grass pitch for klossen, an old-fashioned game).

By and large the above-mentioned designers determined the transition from the type of grand, open landscape park to the eclectic, historical type of park with enclosed spaces. This mixed landscape style was applied on the country estates of the landed nobility, who were in decline, and a new class of rich industrialists. These mixed-style estates, together with the city parks of the first half of the twentieth century and the parks laid out on former town fortifications, especially those designed by father and son Zocher, provide a representative overview of landscaping in the early twentieth century. All this is developed in an archaic way of

working and in archaic labour relationships. Modern inventions were greeted with enthusiasm, but also heralded the end of an era in which nobility and bourgeoisie had a plentiful supply of cheap labour. In the Netherlands, World War I marked its close.

House style and garden style do not always match

During the Renaissance and Baroque periods various disciplines, such as painting, interior design and garden art, would more or less follow the same art styles. In the nineteenth century, eclectic as it was, this was no longer the case until art nouveau once again united the various disciplines. Art nouveau manifested itself less exuberantly in the Netherlands than in the neighbouring countries, perhaps because it was considered a bit too frivolous by the stolid Dutch, who disparagingly called it the 'Salad Oil' style – a reference to a poster in this style made by Jan Toorop for a salad oil manufacturer. With regard to gardens it is more complicated and in architecture, however, there are several examples of more outspoken Jugendstil buildings. Villa Rams Woerthe, in Steenwijk, is one of them. It has many organic design elements, including the art nouveau entrance gate and bridge. But the park was laid out in mixed landscape style after a drawing by Hendrik Copijn. A drive leads straight up to the house, passing a lawn bordered by beds of annuals. Beyond the meandering flowerbeds at the sides of the house lie meadows with clumps of trees. Behind the house a pond along the longitudinal axis of the park divides the park into two long strips. The bridges connecting the two sides are ornamented with motifs in art nouveau style. From the house there is a full view of the park with the perspective broken up by a ha-ha, which is a wet or dry ditch used for separating foreground and background. The ha-ha at Rams Woerthe also fulfils its original purpose, which was to prevent cattle, or in this case deer, from dipping into the flowerbeds. The present deer park is separated from the garden in a rather less subtle fashion, alas, however effective it may be – a wire-mesh fence topped by barbed wire. The house and the park are being restored under the aegis of the European Union, as announced on an enormous, ugly sign at the elegant front gate. It somehow lacks the refinement, characteristic of art nouveau.

Large villas, small gardens

The eastern parts of the Netherlands are naturally more suitable for landscape style gardens than the wetter western part of the country, where much of the reclaimed land is transected by straight canals. The economy was in good shape in the early twentieth century and new ideas about form and nature called for *Gesamtkunstwerke*. Traditional designers working in landscape style, many of whom were used to designing large gardens, watched with Argus' eyes as architects and gardeners, co-operating with young garden architects, developed a new type of country-house in which the garden was 'organically' integrated in the total design. The architect K.P.C. de Bazel was one of the first to express his views on the form and content of the 'outdoor area'. Many modern town villas were built on rather small parcels which left little room for a proper garden design. As a consequence architects began to include the area between the house and the hedge in their designs. In De Bazel's design for a house for the banker van Lanschot for example, in 's Hertogenbosch, the house occupies a quarter of the lot. A drive and some paths and flowerbeds have been sketched around the house. Some of the beds are specified merely as 'bed for summer plants', which would make any landscape architect with a horticultural background blush.

Rural estates become residential neighbourhoods

A new phenomenon in town planning was the residential neighbourhood, or villa park. Many were planned on former country estates, or what remained of them, close to cities as well as in rural areas. Modern comforts and developments like cars were available, while retaining the feel of country life. In towns and villages surrounding the main cities in particular, many such residential areas were built for the rising middle class. Hendrik Copijn and J.D. Zocher, Jr., designed villa parks with the underlying idea that the new villas would require individual garden designs; property developers smartly creating a new market for themselves. The garden architect Dirk Wattez drafted the plan for the residential area Nassaupark, in Bussum, on a former country estate, Het Spiegel. He designed meandering lanes and large villas on relatively small lots, making clever use of existing trees. These were maintained in a great variety of individually laid out gardens. The final result was a leafy neighbourhood with lots of shadow and dark gardens, at an easy walking distance from the railway station.

Japanese gardens in Holland

The Suez canal, faster ships and regular services brought the West and the East into closer proximity, as did the telegraph and World Exhibitions. Baroness van Brienen travelled to the Far East several times in the late nineteenth century and laid out a garden in Japanese style on her Clingendael estate near The Hague. It is certain that Petzold, Springer and both Zochers, the elder and the younger, were involved in re-arranging the original classicist garden, but it is unclear who actually designed the new garden or how the ornaments got to The Hague. Anyway, it became the most important oriental garden in Japanese style in the Netherlands and it can still be viewed today. The lessons the baroness learned on her travels show in moss paths, bridges, a pavilion and suitable vegetation. A spring walk through the rhododendron and azalea lane at the peak of blossom is a breathtakingly colourful experience which shakes all customary notions of harmony and colour. Under the supervision of Th.J. Dinn, who went on to become a garden architect, a nursery was established to grow the appropriate plants.

19

Modern times, modern plants

The Victorian gardens of the nineteenth century were maintained by an army of personnel. There was plenty of time to raise and plant annuals and this was taken into account in the design of the garden. At strategic points like a junction of paths or the end of a vista, round, oval or square beds were made which were planted with different plants each year. A planting plan was drawn up in spring. Often, vertical patterns were applied with bright red, bright white and deep blue annuals at the bottom and plants from the orangery at the top: flowering agapanthuses, palms or agaves. Summer residences, city parks and pleasure gardens were all beautifully arranged. Around the turn of the century major changes set in. Personnel became more expensive; houses became smaller and were more often permanently inhabited. Logically, garden work was streamlined and open-ground perennials were favoured both in private gardens and in public parks. Perennials require less care than annuals, obviously, and annual planting plans were no longer required. The hey-day of what the Germans aptly call Teppichgärtnerei [carpet gardening] was over.

Plant Breeders' Catalogue 1900

The catalogue of the Moerheim nursery in Dedemsvaart for the year 1900 catered for public welfare gardens in particular. Dwarf and climbing French beans were the pride of Bonne Ruys, the owner and founder of the nursery. Thanks to his cosmopolitan upbringing and traineeships abroad, Ruys spoke several languages fluently and knew growers in England, Germany and Denmark personally. He also took a keen interest in new business methods and was the first plant breeder in the Netherlands to use a loose-leaf card system to record plant and customer data. In the vegetable department the catalogue lists many cabbage species, including French and English broccoli, which were virtually unknown in the Netherlands at the time, as well as cucumbers for indoor cultivation, the so-called 'Zimmergurke'. In the flower department many annuals were listed, including dwarf and other types of asters. Anemone japonica 'Honorine Jobert' was already a standard item. Also a page is dedicated to ornamental grasses mentions gunnera (Giant rhubarb) and rheum palmatum (Turkey rhubarb, or Chinese rhubarb).

Gunnera scaba.

Moerheim Catalogue (1900)

21

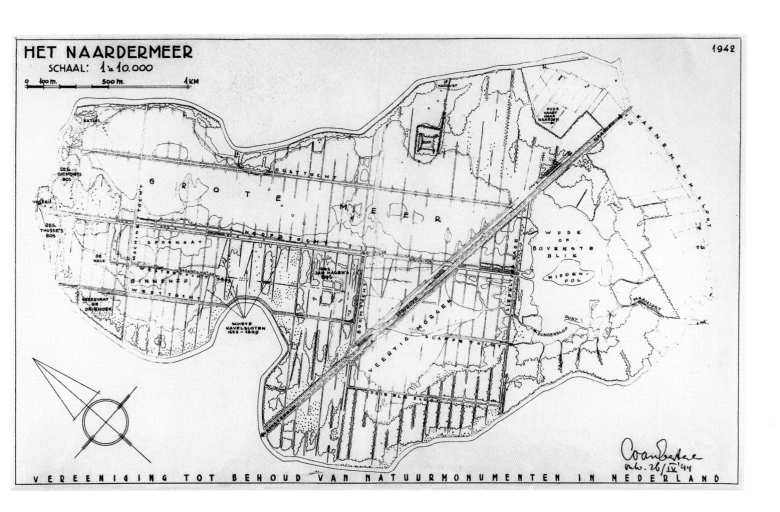

Het Wijde Gat, remainder of the old connection between the river Vecht and the Naardermeer (about 1905)

On the shores of the Naardermeer: the study reservation De Berkenboschjes (about 1905)

Map of the Naardermeer, cut across by the railway line Amsterdam-Hilversum. This is the first purchase by

the Society for the Preservation of Nature (1942)

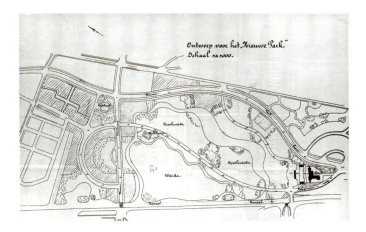

22

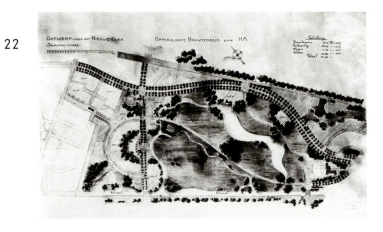

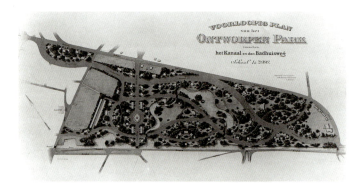

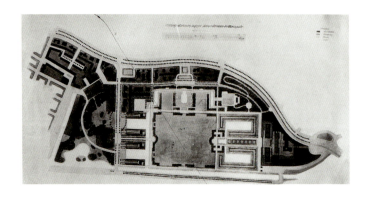

Four different stages of design for the Westbroekpark in The Hague. **L.P. Zocher, P. Westbroek, H.E. Suyver, H.W. Schürmann, S.G.A. Doorenbos** and **N. Roozen** all designed various phases of the development of the park

In the beginning of the twentieth century the allotment garden was the big source of vitamins (situation 2000)

E.F. André and **H.A.C. Poortman** determined the appearance of the gardens round Middachten Castle, De Steeg (Rheden)

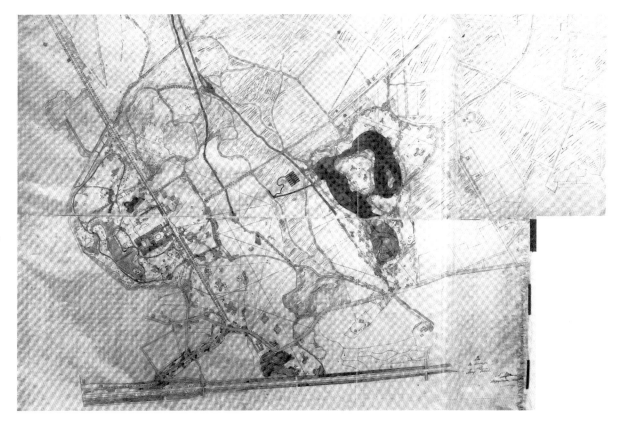

L.P. Zocher, C.E.A. Petzold, E.F. André, H.A.C. Poortman all made designs for Twickel, the largest Dutch country estate in Delden (Ambt Delden) (1900)

Combination of Victorian 'Teppichgärtnerei' in front and English landscape in the background. Duinrell, Wassenaar, early twentieth century

27

C.E.A. Petzold and **H.A.C. Poortman** both designed gardens for Weldam Castle, Goor (1907). The mix of a classicist garden with a nineteenth-century open view of the landscape can be attributed to **E.F. André**

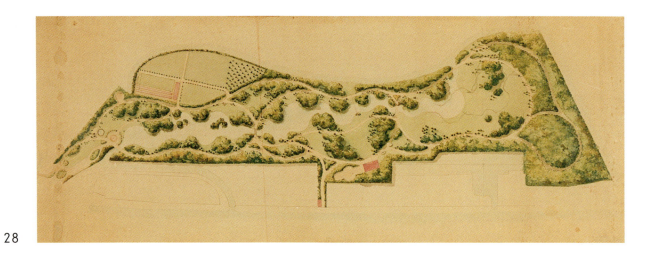

28

H. Copijn Rams Woerthe, Steenwijk (1899)

The Jugendstil-inspired garden decorations, such as this small bridge are in sharp contrast with the design in mixed

garden style of **H. Copijn**, Rams Woerthe, Steenwijk (1899)

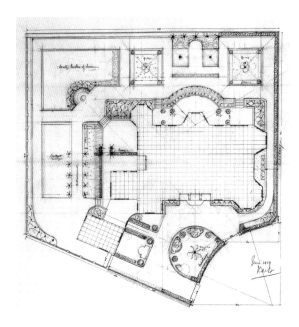

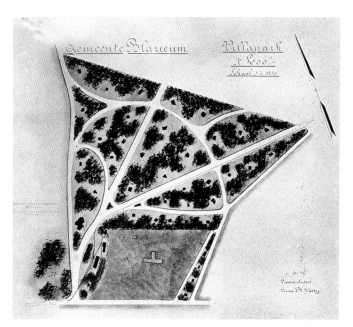

The architect **K.P.C. de Bazel** built an enormous house on a small plot for Mr van Lanschot (1908). At the same time the architect designed the small garden in the remaining space

The ground plan of **K.P.C. de Bazel**'s house determines the shape of Mr van Lanschot's small town garden (1908)

D. Wattez designed villa park 't Loo, new villas in the vicinity of country estates (1879)

K.P.C. de Bazel residence De Maerle and garden for the painter G.W. van Blaaderen, Bussum (1906)

K.C. van Nes bourgeois garden

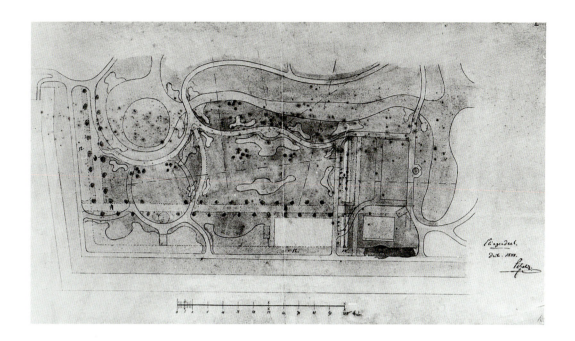

C.E.A. Petzold was the initiator of the design for the Japanese Garden on the country estate Clingendael in Wassenaar (1888)

1910-1920

• New styles • prints provide inspiration • garden village Vreewijk (no pub) • regional work area • organic landscapes and architectural gardening • early attempts to set up a trade association • BNT [Association of Dutch Garden Architects], the beginnings • education, logical • curled endive 'Silberherz'

Prints provide inspiration

For the historical style of garden design prevalent in the late nineteenth century prints and paintings from the early Renaissance provided inspiration. The neo-Renaissance architecture of P.H.J. Cuypers, who built the Rijksmuseum in Amsterdam, carried on into the 'neo' design of the gardens surrounding the museum. The Renaissance style shows in the raised beds centring on a tree or well and the parterres that are sparsely planted and spacious. To see little black sand was quite acceptable. Flowers that were exotic at the time of the Renaissance – tulips, narcissi, marigolds and sunflowers – were planted so that they could be observed from all sides. L.A. Springer was aware of the Renaissance ideas, of course, and undoubtedly took them as the starting point for his plan for an enclosed garden in the Frans Hals Museum in Haarlem (1913). But spacious beds that are empty save for a single flowering plant are not very attractive design material, and so he designed a forecourt with more extensive plantings. The present plantings are a simplified form of his original design; rather a kind of trimmed down variation on a true, if somewhat pale imitation of a Renaissance garden.

Garden village Vreewijk versus Papaverhof

The recreation of a rural atmosphere in urban patterns and the preservation of village community values and along with that social control were two major arguments for building garden villages. The idea was first developed in England by Ebenezer Howard and was applied in the Netherlands in a number of cities, in many different ways. Companies like Stork, Koninklijke Gist and Philips built complete garden villages for their employees, close to their factories in Hengelo, Delft and Eindhoven. Vreewijk in Rotterdam, designed by the architect M.J. Granpré Molière in 1913, was the grandest project of this kind. Narrow streets are lined with small, low-roofed houses built of traditional Dutch brick. The houses have small front gardens, with privet hedges lining pavements punctuated by trees, and larger back gardens with rear access which can be used as kitchen gardens or for pleasure. The plentiful greenery surrounding the homes and a generous sprinkling of public gardens throughout the neighbourhood bring out its residential character, which is emphasized by a village-like quietness. It is remarkable that this project, innovative for its greenery, was planned by an architect. It was Granpré Molière who provided the broad outline, curved vistas along the main axes which link up to the urban functions outside the neighbourhood. It was a common view at the time that people living in garden villages would live better and more moral lives, spending their spare time on sports fields rather than in pubs, and so in 1920 there was not a single pub in the whole of Vreewijk.

A few years later, J. Wils designed the garden village Papaverhof, in The Hague, according to the ideas of De Stijl. Houses, gardens and the public garden in the centre all conform to a strictly geometrical style. The urban, open houses have flat roofs and a cubist look. The fences, flower tubs and the ponds in the park all contribute to the overall impression of strict geometrical orderliness. This time the Howard principle was applied completely different.

Regional top designers: Dirk and Pieter Wattez

Two 'regional' designers worthy of mention are Dirk and Pieter Wattez. Dirk Wattez was a tree nurseryman from Bussum who moved to the Twente region in the eastern part of the country. He worked mainly for textile manufacturers – Van Heek, Ter Kuile, Blijdenstein, Jannink – and designed gardens for country houses like Zonnebeek, De Kotten, De Welle, Het Stroot and Ledeboerpark. He also designed the landscape-style Volkspark in Enschede, the first true working-class park, in which his love of trees is apparent. He loved to use exotic trees like giant sequoias or bright-green large-leaved catalpas, which can be admired to this day – a living testimony to his craftsmanship. Dirk's son Pieter followed in his father's footsteps. For the American lady-owner of Zonnebeek, a villa in white plantation style, he redesigned the layout of the grounds. Working in landscape style at first, his style gradually became more 'angular' and eventually strictly geometrical, as at Huis te Maarn. Both father and son introduced many exotic trees, mainly in Twente, which now seem to fit quite naturally in the landscape.

Organic integration in the landscape

Alice de Stuers, daughter of Victor de Stuers, who was chairman of what became later the Netherlands Department for Preservation of Monuments, is the spiritual mother of the gardens of De Wiersse in the Achterhoek region. When she began to remake the gardens, which had been neglected for some time, she was strongly influenced by the ideas of the English garden designer Gertrude Jekyll, who introduced perennial borders. De Wiersse is a country house nestling beautifully in a system of lanes and meadows surrounded by tall groups of rhododendrons. A brook, the Baakse Beek, protects the house and powers a water mill. An invisible ditch, a fine example of a ha-ha, keeps cattle out of the garden while preserving the view from the house. There is a parterre garden in classical English style with mossy stones, rock plants and a perennial border containing del-phinium, phlox, gypsophila, verbascum and asters. When Alice was only fifteen years old, she laid out the first rose beds, squares of ten-der-coloured roses fenced off by box hedges. The formal garden near the house is connected to the more loosely structured landscape beyond by means of pieces of statuary, placed on visual axes, and birch woods, all embedded in brook scenery carpeted with narcissi in spring. De Stuers' English husband, Major W.E. Gatacre, planned the broad outline of the park. He cleared up visual axes, hid paths behind belts of trees and widened the paths to two metres, a comfortable width for two people to walk side by side. Alice and her husband created a lovely Arcadian landscape with smooth transitions to the house and the formal flower garden. The gardens can be visited in spring when the rhododendrons and azaleas blossom.

Architectural gardening

A characteristic feature of the New Architectural Style of Gardening was the incorporation of all kinds of structures in gardens. Low walls were used to accentuate or bridge differences in level, pergolas to change the perspective or the horizon. Instead of oval ponds with natural banks, rectangular brick-walled basins were constructed to give gardens an orderly appearance, although in some cases this may also appear as wilfully rigid and artificial. The brickwork structure of the Remmerstein villa, designed by D.F. Tersteeg, has been preserved beautifully and still looks very authentic. The house was built 1912 and so has the same age as the garden design. The austere, rectangular layout continues in the pattern of lanes in the surrounding terrain. The private garden is very similar to the garden of hotel De Hooge Vuursche, which is still open to the public. The design of the latter is less austere, in the sense that semicircles can be traced in the drawings. These mirror the semi-circular walls of the castle-like country house, designed by the architect

Eduard Cuypers, which has much symmetrical, harmonious brickwork.

BNT, the first trade association of garden architects

The great landscape architects of the early twentieth century were firmly anchored in the landscape style prevalent in that period and had close ties with many owners of castles and country estates. They felt threatened by the rapid rise of the Nieuwe Bouwen and, with it, the advent of architects who also designed gardens. Professional pride and business interests were at stake and so in 1917 a first attempt was made to set up a trade association to protect their profession. Horticultural education and garden architecture training were regarded as the key instruments for keeping out architects and nurserymen-designers, and strict rules were drawn up accordingly. In 1922, in Hotel Riche in Arnhem, a new association was founded, the Bond van Nederlandsche Tuinarchitecten, BNT [Association of Dutch Garden Architects]. This organization forbade garden architects to use plants from their own nurseries for gardens they designed until 1925. The measure was intended to prevent dumping of surplus begonias and petunias, but in practice it did not benefit the development of the association. The reason is that breeding their own plants, often less current varieties, was essential for many designers to be able to properly execute their designs. Mien Ruys, for example, simply needed the Moerheim nursery to be able to express her ideas properly. The prohibition was withdrawn after three years, but it characterized the narrow-minded, protectionist spirit of the founders of the association. The contrast between 'gardening' architects on the one hand, and town-planning landscape architects on the other, was evident from the first and continued to play a prominent part throughout the history of BNT. The association did useful things too, of course. An important achievement was the establishment of a training course for landscape architects at Wageningen Agricultural College

[now Wageningen University], and in 1940 it held a photo exhibition of BNT members' designs. Unfortunately, the exhibition was overshadowed by the German occupation of the Netherlands in that year, but the BNT has survived to this day.

Education, logical, straight avenues

One of the protagonists of a trade association for garden architects was H.F. Hartogh Heys van Zouteveen, who was a lecturer in Wageningen. He devoted much time to the improvement of horticultural education and wrote his book De Siertuin [The Ornamental Garden] for that purpose. Hartogh Heys had outspoken ideas about gardens, of whatever kind. He abhorred the popular nineteenth century books by Gijsbert van Laar because the garden models shown in these books were applied indiscriminately in new villa gardens, with oval and round flowerbeds brimful of annuals and illogical lane patterns with unnecessary bends. In Hartogh Heys' opinion landscape style had degenerated into a hodgepodge. It was high time to teach a new generation of students proper modern garden design, beginning with the students of the State Horticultural Winter School. A word frequently occurring in Hartogh Heys' book from 1920, which was written for professionals as well as interested laymen, is 'logical'. Roads logically lead from A to B. In flat terrain they are straight, obviously, and in sloping terrain they will curve but do so only in a natural way. Roads should look as if they have always been there. In Hartogh Heys' view, what distinguishes a landscape garden from a 'regular garden' is the pattern of lanes. The layout of the garden depends on the location of the house, which in turn is subject to conditions like wind directions, the position of the sun and the vegetation protecting the house. How are the windows placed, how large are they, is the house raised above the surrounding terrain? Only when all these conditions have been taken into account can we begin to design a garden. Hartogh Heys first lists the possibilities: a house on a sloping river bank, a building on the sea on top of a dune, a garden in open woodland, a city garden, etc. Each type of garden has its particular requirements. Curiously, he seldom mentions the mixed form of landscape style and architectural style, but he does describe a large number of trees and plants, how they should be planted and how they should be maintained.

Plant Breeders' Catalogue 1910

Vegetable gardens are still the main subject in the Moerheim catalogue for 1910. New vegetables offered are cabbage lettuce 'Duke of Cornwall' and late curled endive 'Silberherz'. Besides, common vegetables like chicory, early green peas and black salsify, globe artichokes are also listed. The garden plants section includes many varieties of gerberas, annual poppies, and many varieties of carnations, sweet peas and ornamental tobacco. Campanula persifolia moerheimi is proudly presented, at two guilders for ten. Local attachment is evident in phlox 'Baron van Dedem' and in the offer of epimedium, indigenous plants and so-called manor flora, all grouped together without distinction.

35

Moerheim Catalogue (1910)

36

J. Gratema garden village houses for the building society Eigen Haard in Nieuwendammerham, Amsterdam-Noord

(1918)

J. Wils designed garden village Papaverhof in The Hague in modern style (1919)

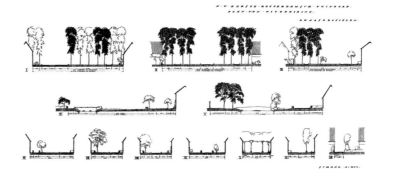

M.J. Granpré Molière in collaboration with **P. Verhagen, J.H. de Roos, W.S. Overeijnder** garden village
Vreewijk, Rotterdam (1916-1919)

P.H. Wattez Zonnebeek, Enschede (1910)

The star-shaped sightlines by **S. Voorhoeve**, in the park Lauswolt still set the scene, even today, Beesterzwaag (1928)

39

D.F. Tersteeg garden, Bussum

D.F. Tersteeg Hooge Vuursche, Baarn (1910)

D.F. Tersteeg   Remmerstein, Rhenen (1912)

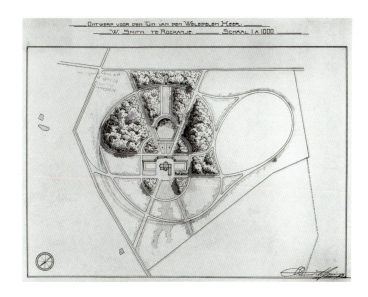

L.A. Springer   design for the Rotterdam port tycoon W. Smith Olaertsduyn, Rockanje (Westvoorne) (1910)

Alice de Stuers designed the rose garden for De Wiersse, Vorden (1912-1928)

• Lady gardeners • Mien Ruys, grande dame of Dutch gardening • 'De Stijl' garden in Drachten • planning the new Wieringermeer Polder • Springer c.s. versus Van Nes: landscape garden or architectural style? • imitation rocks in the Utrecht hills • new master, new garden • candid contrasts • Moerheim has a 'department for garden architecture'

Mien Ruys

Apart from the emancipation of garden architecture as a profession, another form of emancipation also took place: women entered the profession. Once again England led the way, that is, Gertrude Jekyll, the 'mother' of the traditional border, did. The first lady gardener of renown in the Netherlands was Mien Ruys, who grew up on her father's nursery Moerheim (house on the moors), in Dedemsvaart, in a place where designers landscaping the large country estates still placed their orders in French. Mien's father, Bonne Ruys, inspected his crops and directed his employees in the fields on horseback. During his lifetime Bonne Ruys crossed and introduced a large number of perennials. Popular plants such as phlox 'Rosa Spier' and astilbe 'Professor van der Wielen' are still for sale, and sunflower 'Moerheim Beauty' and monkshood 'Ruysii Pink Sensation' brighten gardens to this day. Mien Ruys was more interested in what to do with all these plant species. When still a girl she was given a garden of her own in which she experimented with shade plants and semi-naturalization. She was not only interested in flowers, but also studied leaf shapes, capsules, pappi, and colour changes in autumn. She was intrigued by modern architectural ideas, which can be summarized as 'light, space and fresh air', and developed a love for architectural garden and landscape design. She would start from a proper right-angled ground plan defined by hedges and paving, and then fill in the plants, predominantly perennials. Ruys' preference for this form also shows in her use of shade plants, which was revolutionary at the time. To explain her ideas she laid out experimental gardens in Dedemsvaart after 1925, which still inspire generations of garden lovers to this day. After World War II her 'ready-made' borders of 10x2, 5x2 and 3x1 metres, which were a great success. Variation in the borders depended on the type of soil and their location in relation to the sun. Mien Ruys liked to experiment with materials alien to gardens. Her use of railway sleepers (from railway lines that had fallen into disuse) to mark off beds earned her the nickname 'Sleeper Mien'. She replaced natural flagstones with mass-produced washed gravel flagstones, turned upside down, and in general influenced the layout of many home gardens. Frequently imitated, she had great influence on the modern, contemporary garden.

'De Stijl' garden in Drachten

The early twentieth century saw many new artistic styles and movements, some of which had more impact than others. One of the more lasting movements was De Stijl, and one of the most prominent representatives was Theo van Doesburg. De Stijl stood for abstract, geometrical designs without ornamentation. In his plans for public housing in Drachten, Theo van Doesburg included even the smallest details, not forgetting the gardens. In each garden the centrepiece is a garden vase of his own design. The proportions of these vase sculptures, which consist of four right-angled columns of varying height, were calculated according to a strict numerical order (16-12-10-8-6-4-2). The vases are very effective from all sides, not least because of their neutral colours, white-and-grey and black-and-grey. Around the central vase van Doesburg planned flowerbeds for which he initially indicated only the primary colours, in the proportion eight parts blue, five parts red and three parts yellow. Around these beds he planned flower-beds in the same colours mixed with evergreens flowering in violet and purple. Finding the plants to fit the colour scheme was a minor consideration to van Doesburg, one which he was happy to leave to his wife, Nelly van Doesburg. Here, the artist reduced nature to the role of supplying the colours and filling in the surfaces of a typical De Stijl design.

The many-sided Tine Cool

Tine Cool's place in the gardening scenes is more sensitive and confused. A woman in a men's world, she had to suffer patronizing reviews like, 'We note that this is the work of a young woman and that many young women nowadays feel attracted to garden architecture. Work like hers, such detailed attention for the atmosphere created by smaller plants, is typical of feminine sensibilities.' Tine Cool was indeed deeply interested in the character of flowering plants. She endeavoured to make a sea of flowers look as exuberant as possible and to make it bloom throughout the seasons for as long as possible. She regarded a connection between indoors and outdoors as essential and advocated large windows and easy-to-open garden doors. Cool travelled widely, published books and articles and acted as a judge. She designed gardens in close consultation with her clients. It gave her joy to help garden lovers make the right choice of plants and find well-balanced colour combinations. In her view gardens ought to radiate a peaceful atmosphere, highlights of colour and fragrance alternating with quieter sections. Cool's writings were as varied as her designs. She wrote a girl's book Met z'n vijven naar Rome as well as a book on flower myths and legends Bloemen-mythen en legenden in which she identified the relationships between humans, trees and herbs. From Lady's Slipper to Devil's Dung.

Lost in the garden

Wandering through the lesser-known parts of the Dutch gardening landscape, from the intuitive Tine Cool we arrive at the metaphorical C.M. van Hille-Gaerthé, who published a book titled Tuintjes [Small Gardens] in 1922; it contains three stories, Voorjaars-Hofje, Kindertuintjes and De Man en zijn Tuin [Spring Garden, Children's Gardens and The Man and his Garden]. The stories do not deal with these subjects in any horticultural sense, however, as the following sample of van Hille's highly sensitive prose, from De Man en zijn Tuin, may serve to demonstrate.

'Yesterday late, as the flowers stood like silent spirits in the still evening, he had stood there for a long time contemplating them. If I were a composer, he mused, I would compose them into a song of chiming bells, a symphony of life; the soft sound of the wide white bells I would transform into the timid tones of happy, unspoilt youth; the ringing of the pinkish red, lilac and blue calyxes would express budding life, strong and beautiful in maturity, but also darkened towards sadness and passion and sin.' Bellflowers, evidently, provided the inspiration, plucked by the husband and presented to a visiting lady-friend. Reminiscing he continues, 'When the grass had not yet been sown, Elisa and himself had once, on a glorious September day during their engagement period, stood in this same barren garden. He had shown her his plan for the garden, pointing out the imaginary plants. Look, here at the sunny side we shall plant spring flowers, daphne and wallflowers, with a handful of tulips strewn among them. The summer plants will be a little deeper into the garden, poppies and columbines in all hues and colours; and right at the back near the fence we will have huge sunflowers. Near the shed a row of rigid, paper-dry hollyhocks, with scarlet geraniums hanging from the roof.' I will not disclose the outcome, but the garden gave the man all the solace he needed.

Planning the Wieringermeer Polder

The reclamation of the Wieringermeer was the first large-scale landscaping project of the twentieth century. A completely new landscape was to take shape, an immense task for the planners. 'Virginal land is to be transformed into habitable land which must also have its share of beauty. People should not spend their whole lives living in utilitarian buildings,' the spokesman for the Zuiderzee Project Authority, V.J.P. de Blocq van Kuffeler, generously wrote in a brochure issued by the Commercial Propaganda Bureau. The Netherlands have a centuries-old tradition of land reclamations. What was new in the case of the Wieringermeer was that, besides agriculture first, and waterways, roads and towns second, other factors, to be supervised by experts, were also taken into account in planning the new landscape. Still, the final result was typically Dutch. The plans drawn up by the architect Granpré Molière, an experienced town planner who was asked to make a first draft in 1927, were quite traditional with red-tiled roofs, church spires and straight roads lined with rows of trees to catch the wind. All in all a practical agricultural landscape was shaped, suited to a hard-working farming population. J.T.P. Bijhouwer, who was engaged by the Forestry Commission in 1931, had a more thorough approach. He made studies of types of farm buildings and of wind intensities in summer and winter. Based on these studies he proposed low protective vegetation, roadside trees and protective groups of trees around farms, something he took a particular interest in. Farmyards were laid out with work in mind, and so the vegetable garden and the dunghill were located with an eye to convenience. Plantings in the villages did not need to be as functional and were planned more loosely. The planning of the Wieringermeer, which meant setting up a new agricultural society, proved to be a useful starting point for later landscaping projects on reclaimed land.

Landscape or town garden?
The late mixed landscape style often applied by garden architects such as Springer, Petzold and Poortman remained a subject for debate in the Netherlands for a long time. These men transformed scores of country estates into park-like landscapes with meandering paths, solitary trees, and some kind of classical garden, or at least a flower garden with geometrical flowerbeds, the garden usually being situated near the house. The new villa parks and the larger town gardens demanded a wholly different approach. Many architects not only designed the house but also planned the garden, as an extension of the architectural concept of the house, including the traditional visual axes. The garden architect K.C. van Nes, like many colleagues before him, added fuel to the fire by publicly asking the question whether garden architects were able to design villa parks and, conversely, whether architects should be allowed to design planting plans for gardens. The concept 'landscape architect' was debated over and over again, and what exactly the competence of such an architect should be. Both Springer, who represented the large country estates, and van Nes, who represented modern garden architecture, realized that there was a major task for a designer who could make a comprehensive plan for the entire area. If necessary with infrastructure like roads and railroads included. In his own garden designs van Nes took the environment into account and would either make a design in harmony with it or deviate radically. He also had regard for regional plants and trees. He was not afraid to hide buildings he thought ugly from sight completely by planting clusters of trees. Once again he highlighted the debate on the large landscape-style garden and the architectural villa garden.

Town gardens: 'nothing special'
In the 1920s town gardens were not 'pleasure gardens' as we know them now. Towns were still relatively small and the countryside was not far away. In summer the wealthy retreated to their country houses and the working classes at best had an allotment garden supplied by the Society for Public Welfare. Yet there was beauty hidden behind the façades of houses situated on canals. In 1925 a landscape gardeners' company, Corona, brought out a brochure with

photographs of such town gardens saying, 'It is commonly thought that town gardens (meaning gardens in towns which are usually situated behind or in between houses) are "nothing special"; a nice spot perhaps but a place where nothing will grow, so that the name of "garden" hardly applies. This common notion is quite wrong, however. It has probably taken hold because most people do not know of the beautiful plants and gardens hidden behind some houses, while only a few people have had the opportunity to see these with their own eyes.' The brochure shows pictures of gardens laid out by Corona. The designs vary from large town gardens with meandering paths and flowerbeds with annuals to architectural gardens with right-angled retaining walls.

Imitation rocks in the Utrecht hills

For a long time zoos were among the most unnatural of places for observing animals. By modern standards only simple deer parks, which were often part of a larger park, might qualify as parks. Ouwehands Dierenpark in Rhenen, built as an imitation of other zoos, was no exception to the rule. A relatively large number of buildings was packed onto a small area so that visitors did not have far to walk to see the animals, which in turn were packed into small cages. The shape of many buildings was reminiscent of follies, pandas sleeping in pagodas and chamois clambering over chalets. The only green areas in these parks were near the entrance, and the garden terraces, where one could sip one's tea under the trees and admire the Victorian flowerbeds. When the zoo in Rhenen was first expanded the cramped situation of the captive animals was improved. More space was created to make the animals and their environment look more natural. Lianas and artificial rocks made of concrete were introduced, a first step toward the modern zoo with its mini-biotopes, where visitors can walk through tropical butterfly greenhouses and watch bears from the safety of high footbridges.

New master, new garden

Huys ten Donck has been the property of the Groeninx van Zoelen family for centuries, if not continuously. This stately home, facing a river, dates back to the eighteenth century. The wood behind the house is progressively encroached on by new housing estates, sodium lighting and power pylons. The once quiet country lane on top of the river embankment was raised to modern standards of safe height and separates the grounds from the riverside garden and the private landing stage. In summer the inhabitants of the house could (and still might) easily sail to Rotterdam to run their office. The garden and the house have been modified and beautified continually. At one time the garden was turned into a showcase of vases, some of them of very fine quality, garden sculptures, a true pyramid and a ruin. In 1924 L.A. Springer was asked to rearrange the park in accordance with the wishes of the then owner, esquire Groeninx van Zoelen. The two men corresponded extensively about the family grave, the farmstead and the ruin. Exchanging books as well as plant lists, they did not only discuss acer and gleditschia but also Marx, the Soviet Union and the rise of Nazism in the 1930s, for the correspondence was carried on for ten years. The horticultural result of their gentlemanly exchanges was a number of changes in the landscape-style park. The terrain around the farm, the graveyard and the garden across the road were replanted and a more formal garden with rose beds was created near the house. Today, the quiet country lane has become a very busy road, the riverside garden has grown over and there is no longer a free view of the river from the house.

Candid contrasts

Garden architects, whether they work in landscape style or in architectural style, each in their own way take the surrounding landscape into regard and either 'fit in' the landscape or create an intimate garden. In either case they endeavour to create a connection or a distinctive separation between the 'hard' structure

and the 'soft' vegetation around. But not always:
in the case of the sanatorium Zonnestraal, in
Hilversum, one has no sense of connection or
separation whatsoever thanks to its location in
the woods with its fresh air. It is a social monument to the fight against tuberculosis as well as
a wonderful piece of architecture with Bauhaus
influences. The undisguised pride of the makers
reflects on its surroundings. The white building
with its many windows contrasts sharply with
the woods and heath surrounding it. The open
space between the pine trees was not made into
a gradual transition zone, nor is it connected to
either the building or the woods. This structure

46 is somewhat confrontational to an unprepared
walker emerging from the woods.

Plant Breeders' Catalogue 1920

Mien Ruys started to work at her father's
nursery, now 'Royal Moerheim'. She introduced
a special Department for Garden Architecture.
The number of pages listing perennials and
roses had increased significantly and a tree
nursery is mentioned. 'We offer elementary
advice: Unlike potted plants and bulbous plants,
perennials are not suitable for flowerbeds. They
are more suitable for planting in the shelter of
hedges', etc. Customer relations were important
and customers could order or seek advice in five
languages apart from Dutch; in French, English,
German, Danish or Swedish, through P.O. Box
no. 5 or telephone no. 5, girobank account no. 5.
Campanula persicifolia moerheimi is still on
special offer in 1920, and ten astilbes can be
had for the price of eight. The perennials include
mombretia and hemerocalli. The nursery is par-
ticularly proud of its silver-white delphiniums.
Many varieties of rhododendrons and azaleas
are on offer and a full page is reserved for an
illustration of the conifer Picea pungens moerheimi, a new variety bred at the nursery.

Moerheim Catalogue (1920)

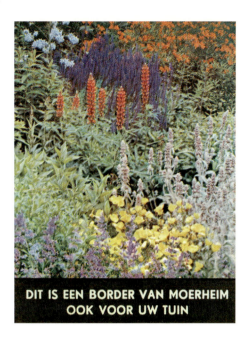

DIT IS EEN BORDER VAN MOERHEIM
OOK VOOR UW TUIN

Brochure for ordering packages for borders

M. Ruys experimental gardens, Dedemsvaart (1925)

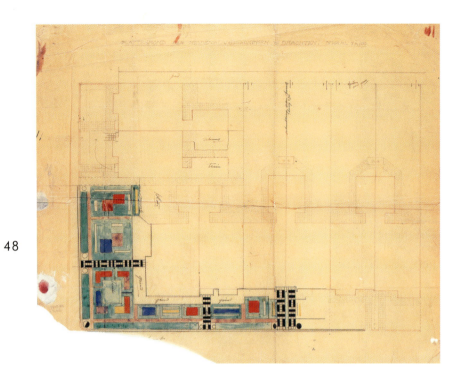

48

Th. van Doesburg garden design for houses, Drachten (1921)

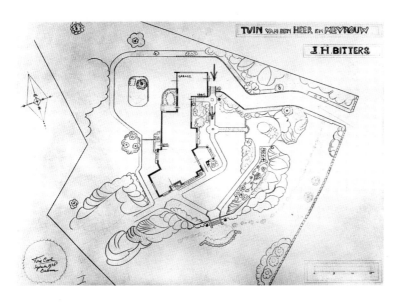

T. Cool garden for Mr J.D. Cremers, Bussum (about 1921)

T. Cool garden for Mr and Mrs J.H. Bitters, Bussum (1938)

T. Cool etching 'The Amaryllis' (1921)

50

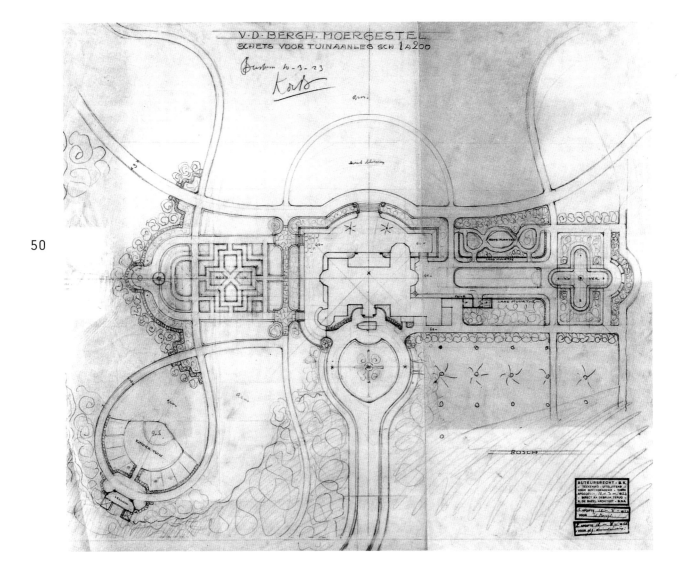

K.P.C. de Bazel   residence and garden for Mr A. van den Bergh, Moergestel (1922)

Garden Daelen-Kolff in Bloemendaal, about 1929

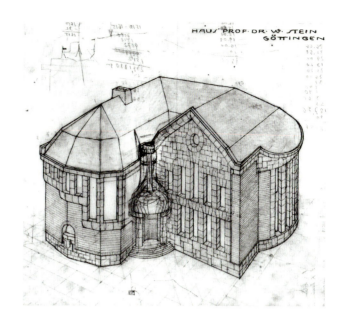

51

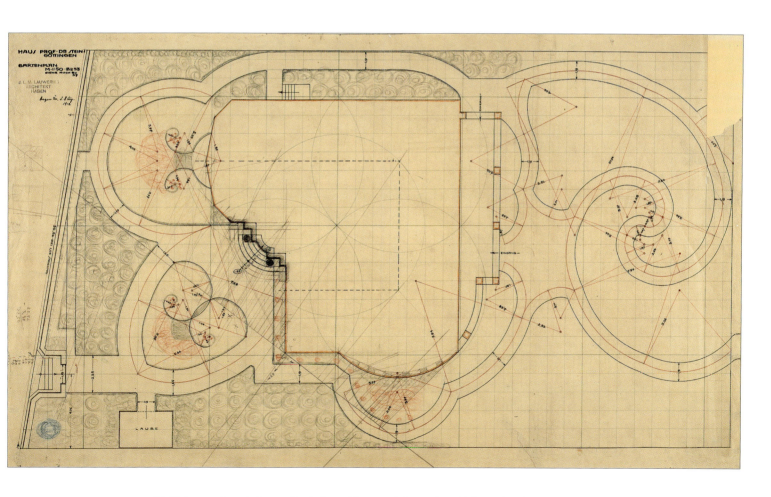

J.L.M. Lauweriks   designer of both the residence and the garden with Jugendstil themes for Prof. Dr. W. Stein,

Göttingen (1912)

52

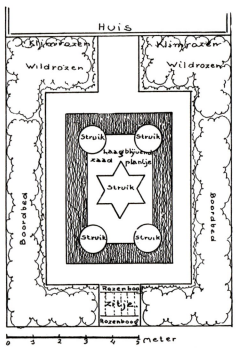

Afb. XII. Regelmatig ingedeelde tuin, beplant met veel rozen.
Het middenvak kan beter met niet één soort rozen of gemengde rozen,
welke even hoog blijven, beplant worden.

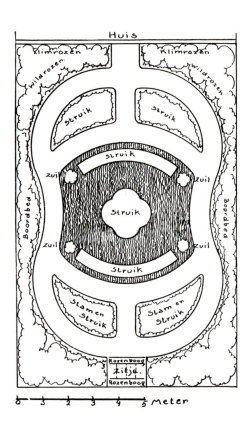

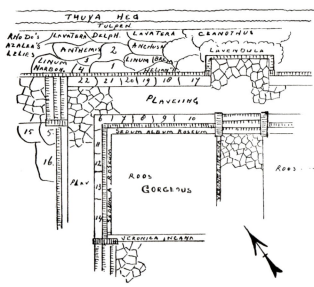

AFB. 113. COMBINATIE VAN GEPLAVEIDE PADEN MET STAPELMUURTJES EN VERDIEPTE
ROZENTUIN.   Tuinarchitect W. N. Lindeman.   Zie afb. 98 en 99 pag. 171.

Beplanting: 1 Paeonia.   2 Anemone jap. H. Joubert.   3 Campanula acaulis.   4 Helianthemum.   5 Tulpen.
6 Oxalis adenophylla.   7 Primula Wanda.   8 Oxalis.   9 Primula veris elatior.   10 Helianthemum.
11 Yucca.   12 Oxalis en Narsissus.   13 Primula veris elatior.   14 Oxalis.   15 Nepeta Mussini.
16 Dianthus plumarius.   17 Saxifraga.   18 Plumbago.   19 Oenothera Missouriensis.   20 Crocus sativa.
21 Tulipa Kaufmanniana.   22 Arabis alpina fol. var.

Gardens with regular patterns

Th.J. Dinn   example of paved paths with stone walls and sunk rose garden

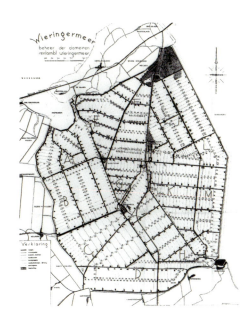

M.J. Granpré Molière, F. Ligtenberg reclamation plan Wieringermeer Polder; **J.T.P. Bijhouwer, G.A. Overdijkink**

planting Wieringermeer Polder (1929-1931)

Middenmeer, Wieringermeer Polder (situation in 1996)

K.C. van Nes   garden for Mr A.E. Dinger, Heerlen (1923)

Th.J. Dinn   the Stroot, Enschede (1925)

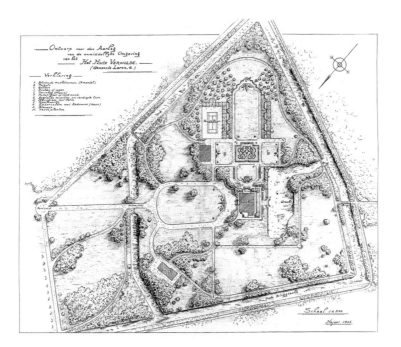

H.A.C. Poortman   the Huis Verwolde, town of Laren (1926)

Dike, garden and the Huys ten Donck in Slikkerveer, early twentieth century

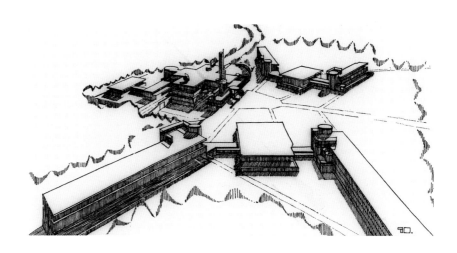

56

J. Duiker, J.G. Wiebenga sanatorium Zonnestraal, Hilversum (1926-1931)

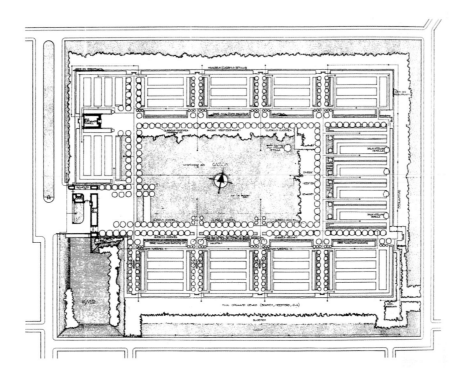

W.M. Dudok entrance building and ground plan Noorderbegraafplaats, Hilversum (1927)

• The architect of home and garden • Boschplan, jewel in the crown of Amsterdam • Bleeker: walls are always ugly • garden layout in accordance with aesthetics • the Sonneveld House and garden • Bijhouwer's perspective • the Limburg botanical garden by Bergmans • garden districts in the style of Modern Living • Bingerden still on the move • These are dark times, do not neglect your garden!

The architect of home and garden

The dual function of designer of both the house and the garden is not unusual. In particular, when a garden style is concerned which we may call 'architectural'. A fine example was J.P. Fokker. First an architect, graduated from Delft University, he developed into a polyvalent maker of Gesamtkunstwerke. Fokker designed homes and gardens as if they were Siamese twins. The house was an inseparable part of its surroundings and the garden was unimaginable as anything but the shell round the house. The view from inside through the French windows of the outside determined the 'axis' in the garden. Being an architect, he concentrated on the art of garden layout and he held strong views on the subject. His love for plants was also evident from his own nursery, De Duinvoet, where the majority of his plants are indigenous. Later he co-operated with Cees Sipkes, an expert on wild plants, in his nursery De Teunisbloem. Fokker was pleased with the co-operation, he was in the first place an architect and didn't want to sneak work from the garden architect. Later on he worked on his own again. Sipkes was the botanist who later reaped fame with his book Wildeplantentuinen [Wild Flower Gardens], and his orchids near the Tenellaplas in Oostvoorne. In the series Moderne Schoonheid [Modern Beauty] Fokker's book Tuinen in Holland [Gardens of Holland] is published by Kosmos in 1932. In itself this was a splendid example of the art of printing. Designed in the style of the Amsterdam School and the magazine Wendingen, the book showed garden designs by young architects, with an abundance of black-and-white photographs, an expensive exercise in those days. In an extensive introduction Fokker explained his philosophies concerning materials, form and planting. Occasionally his vision moved rather strongly in the direction of stone. In an article in the daily paper, the NRC, a critic deplored the label 'natural' being bestowed on lifeless stonewalls rather than on buxus hedges. From the above you will have deduced that in Fokker's garden designs many fossilized shapes can be found, as they can be found in the present Europapark in Gronsveld in Limburg. Initially intended as a private garden, named Klokke Roeland, to form a whole with a house yet to be built, a system of garden walls and pergolas round an octagonal pond was born. The planting consists of many species of roses, fruits and rock plants. Today the park is called Europatuin and forms part of a restaurant chain. There are big plans for renovation of this park, which essentially is an original Fokker garden.

The Amsterdam Woods

Between 1880 and 1930 the population of Amsterdam doubled. A stay in clean open air and contact with nature counterbalanced 'the hectic pace of those who have to make their living in the modern metropolis'. This is a quote from the introduction in the catalogue for the Boschplan, situated close to town to enable school children to spend a free afternoon in the woods. And labourers and office workers without a car could enjoy a beautiful summer evening after work. For the first time in Dutch history a large-scale nature plan was realized for the purpose of combining recreation and nature. Playing sports could be combined with looking for peace and quite and bird watching. A multi-form Boschplan Committee studied countless possibilities based on types of soil, water levels and the users' wishes. Providing jobs for a thousand men during five years was one of the main reasons for this set-up. The plan was presented and approved.

The internal design, made by Cornelis van Eesteren and Jacoba Mulder of the Town Planning Department, served as the basis. The designers advocated the modern, austere straightness of the polder, but they still reverted to the traditional undulating landscape as well. A lot of forest, about half of the nine hundred hectares, alternated with open lawns and water basins. The southern part was intended for quiet relaxation, whereas in the north water sports enthusiasts dominated the scene. There was variation in open and closed and in high and low, too. 'Beauty in diversity.'

The planting was selected for either a quick result or slow growth. In the short term hawthorn, the Guelder rose and the hazel could be enjoyed. Slow growers are oaks and linden trees. In addition, some space was reserved for exotic trees in a special arboretum with educational motives. There was also an ornamental garden, an open-air theatre, a labyrinth and many other green park elements. Never before had such a huge project with such great diversity been launched in the Netherlands. To conclude, another, somewhat overblown, quote from the exhibition catalogue: 'The completed Boschplan will put the missing jewel into the crown of Amsterdam.'

'The Art of Gardening' according to Bleeker

In his book Tuinkunst, het ontwerpen en tekenen van kleine villatuinen **[The Art of Gardening, Designing and Drafting Small Villa Gardens], garden architect G. Bleeker argued that the style of landscaping is highly unsuitable for smaller gardens. He himself started as an employee in Springer's bureau and developed his skills over the years, striking out 'on a modern course'. His ideas**

developed correspondingly. In small gardens a slightly more architectural approach to the planting would be much more suitable. Meandering paths in gardens of modern houses were an abomination to him. All this can be found in his ten basic rules for garden design. Rubble used for garden walls did not find favour with him either. And flagstones provide a false sort of romanticism in a straight-lined garden. Walls were ugly by definition and often covered with plants, preferably useful trained fruit trees. And in modern gardens the natural quality was completely lacking. They were simple in line, design and planting. Small villa gardens were often seen in bright, sunny homes, built for the well-to-do, who have both the money and the inclination to hire a garden architect. Bleeker designed many such gardens. The room taken up by the drive and the garage is amazing. The new 'sacred cow', the automobile, is stabled in all its glory and, if necessary, half the garden is sacrificed to accommodate a drive to an underground garage. Bleeker's list of clients shows that the actual job result is its best promotion. As many as fifty of his garden designs can be found in Haarlem and it surroundings. It is safe to call him a specialist in gardens on sand dunes. A wall provided shelter; if not, Bleeker would put rush screens round the garden to allow Austrian firs time to grow. A list of plants shows traditional planting with snapdragon, marigold, verbena, zinnia and petunia. Besides, dahlias in many colours. Roses are selected according to their flowering until night frost arrives in autumn.

The aesthetics of the garden

In 1938 the book Tuinen **[Gardens] by G.J. Pannekoek and J.J. Schipper told us that laying out a garden 'should always follow the rules of aesthetics'. 'In a work of art systematically pursued proportions should prevail, and a certain ratio between the main parts and the secondary parts and between these and the whole is compulsory.' In actual practice: two thirds lawns and paths and one third plants. All parts of the**

layout should be logical and in exactly the right place and possess a raison d'être. Aesthetics were pursued in every detail. If the house is of good architecture, it is necessary to emphasize this by creating an 'axis'. If the house is a little ragged, then let climbers and clematis grow and in this way the garden will automatically fit the house. The prevailing style was the combination of landscape gardening for larger areas and an architectural, rather austere approach for small gardens. All intermediate forms and combinations were acceptable. So, relegated to the past was the 'garden with its tall standing timber, the frequently sun-starved garden of the end of the

nineteenth century. The contemporary garden matches the current necessities of life and has become the recreational garden; the garden where one can enjoy the sunshine to the full, where the spatial proportions are essential and planting is adapted accordingly.' And the red-brown 'Weser sandstone' still reigns supreme; the flagstones are popular.

Another new development was the reference to the principal in the plan, always mentioned by his full name. A new development was the front garden in towns. In the twentieth century small gardens were laid out in front of houses for the first time. According to Pannekoek this was 'to ensure that the house as a structure is shown to its best advantage. The path to the front door is decisive. This path should lead straight to the house, at least in most town gardens, without any unnecessary detours.'

The unity of the Sonneveld House and garden

With its restoration in 2001, the garden of the Sonneveld House in Rotterdam was largely restored to its original state of 1932. It is a fine example of the organic combination of home and garden fashionable in the thirties that can still be visited today. In many places the open design of the house fits in with the easily accessible garden: they virtually merge into each other. The block-like structure of the house is continued in the green lawn and the taut ever-

green hedges. The varied garden lies farther away from the house. Near the edges of the property the seasons are more noticeable. There are architectural elements in the garden, such as walls, terraces and a fence; they also help to set the severe nature of the garden. The location of the garage at the back of the house is quite remarkable. This solution demands a lot of space for the turning circle and takes up a considerable part of the garden. Apparently they did not feel the need for the largest possible garden area. It seems the car was worth every square inch required for its accommodation and played a prominent part in daily life.

Bijhouwer's perspective

It is interesting to contemplate the problems garden designers had in the thirties in visualizing their ideas and in presenting them to their principals. Nowadays, buyers of a house still on the drawing board can already walk through their virtual garden. They can even see what their garden will look like ten years later. The growth of trees, shrubs and hedges has been calculated on the cad-cam computer. In 1938 things were a lot easier. The generally known Bijhouwer wrote a book and made some sketches: how to visualize a garden and to show to the designer himself and therefore to the client, from the perspective of a frog and a bird's eye view, how the plants will probably develop. It starts with the analysis of the eye and finishes with the various methods used to embellish and colour a drawing. A labour intensive drudgery precedes the presentation of the design. It certainly is awe-inspiring seeing these laborious methods developing into a result opening up new horizons. On the other hand, it should be mentioned that the social status of most designers was such that they could spend all day on their views. Servants would bring them a cup of tea at the right moments and were sure to put in the correct amount of sugar. Until well after World War II this book remained a standard work at the faculty for landscape architects in Wageningen. The latest edition of

Perspectiefconstructie zonder verteekening voor tuin-ontwerpers [**Perspective Construction without Distortion for Garden Designers**] was published in 1966.

Bergmans' botanical garden in Limburg

In the thirties there were vast differences between the regions. For instance, students at the several agricultural colleges in Limburg had to travel to the botanical gardens in Leiden or in Amsterdam to do their practical period. To a number of local politicians this was more than they could take and they started a lobby to build a botanical garden of their own in Kerkrade. In Limburg this meant one had to secure the support of both the church and the mining company. A 'green' pastor still had some land and John Bergmans, a very dynamic man with many publications to his name, made a design in 1938. Bergmans was a member of the Association of Dutch Garden Architects and of the Dutch Dendrology Society and wrote ten classics on the subject of landscaping. Especially in the southern part of Limburg this architect left his mark in many gardens. Surprisingly, beside hundreds of gardens he also designed open-air theatres, zoos and arboreta including the one in Kalmthout. He knew more about growing on loessial soil than anyone. He was a real plant man. His designs followed the selection of plants. Now, the botanical garden in Limburg is listed as a national monument with a big pond, borders with perennials, botanical collections, tub plants, a greenhouse and theme gardens, partly in English and architectural style. In Terwinselen the botanical garden still is in largely the same state in which it was created by Bergmans in 1938. In particular, the meandering path through the valley of conifers is typical of his style. His favourite grey flagstones, rather than the commonly used red variety, grace the ground. He was very keen on rock gardens, dry walls and paths of red brick and he preferred to plants narrow borders for shrubs or hedges. Existing trees were allowed to stay as much as

possible. If any new trees had to be brought in, then small groups of frail birches would be chosen. His great interest in several varieties of heather and conifers (the dwarf variety is ideally suited to a small town garden) fits this picture perfectly. He was the first to devote a complete book to the rock garden. His lists of plants are very accurate and have been consulted by garden architects as their planting bible for many years.

Landscaping with a serving nature

In Hilversum W.M. Dudok built a new town hall in the style of the Nieuwe Bouwen. A large building with horizontal and vertical elements was constructed on the site of a former country estate. The building, with an American touch, inspired by the horizontal designs of Frank Lloyd Wright, was fitted into the existing scenery as far as was possible. The linear shapes in the architecture continued in the long and narrow beds or tubs with their brightly coloured plants. The austere structural lines are softened by the old trees on the former estate and the proud building is reflected in the ponds. The architect, Dudok, gave a great deal of thought to fitting the design into the existing scenery. As was customary in those days, the selection of plants was left to the local Parks and Public Gardens Department. In fact, here the open space planners served the architecture in every detail. 'They must allow the building to rise from the flowers.' Berlage created a similar total picture when he created the Municipal Museum in The Hague. The space outside was made fully subservient by the architect, to underline the geometric aspect of the building. Big ponds have been built reflecting the building and offering a fine view from the covered entrance area. An inside garden, in taut lines, fits the building perfectly.

Garden quarter in 'New Living' style

Amsterdam needed many new houses to replace those in the old quarters in the town centre. These old houses no longer met the requirements, neither in quality nor in quantity. Business activities in the town slowly shifted to the west and town expansion moved with them. The spirit of the times demanded many new houses with the appropriate amenities. In 1934 the Nieuwe Wonen [New Living] architect, C. van Eesteren, designed the urban expansion plan for Amsterdam. His design for its green garden suburbs in the west had a town-like quality: light, air and plenty of green spaces. Flat buildings were placed on strips of land, one behind the other, with green belts between them. The area looks spacious, almost empty. At the time, it must have given the residents, who, before, had been packed together with not a tree in sight, a feeling of luxury. In the new western districts of Amsterdam a lot of green spaces are nearby. Green belt parks and woods or water, created between the new residential areas, extend deep into the town. There are many recreational facilities. Spacious sports parks and a larger, new Sloterplas make the modern worker feel he lives in the country enjoying prosperity and good fortune. For cars there are ample facilities, such as semi-motorways, for instance the Cornelis Lelylaan, where a tram also runs taking its passengers to the town centre near the Bijenkorf on the Dam Square in fifteen minutes.

Bingerden still on the move

Country estates are good criteria for landscape architecture. Most estates do not lead the way when it comes to modernization or streamlining the landscape. The estate owner's close ties with his land often has saving qualities. Groups of trees or solitary trees in the middle of the farmland are saved because of their scenic beauty. The same can be said about windbreaks and hawthorn hedges. This fairly conservative attitude has also led to many indigenous plants seeking asylum on country estates where they can thrive quietly. This is what we see on Bingerden. The van Weede family have lived on the estate for centuries and they are committed to the task of passing the estate on from generation to generation. To do this one has to be aware of the rules and regulations at all administrative levels. One has to know the Nature Protect-ion Act. Attacks by the Betuwelijn project and motorways have to be repelled. Rivers that are allowed to go their own way again are not always a blessing for the water level on the adjacent estates. Up till now Bingerden has managed to survive all flooding, occupation and fire. Its landscape has lived through centuries of development and the residents can be proud of the result we see today. The scenic landscape of the Achterhoek is home to the farms. Nearer the house the hill, the austere garden, the vegetable garden and several borders are the result of centuries of planning. Started round 1800 by the designer J.P. Posth and later C.E.A. Petzold, the estate became the subject of plans for reorganization by S. Voorhoeve in 1935. It all turned out differently and visitors walking on the lawns on 'open house' days today do so in blissful ignorance.

Plant Breeders' Catalogues 1930 and 1932

The first catalogue to appear after the stock exchange crash in 1929, still radiated optimism. There was a growing number of recommendations in the 1930 catalogue of the Moerheim nursery, advice with pictures about pruning roses, care of shrubs and rhododendrons, four pages showing conifers. In the list of perennials a pre-selection was made: groundcovers, plants suitable for city gardens, shade plants, plants for marshes and for dry soil. Apart from the familiar delphinium and phlox there was a separate list with 'new and rare perennials'. The erica carnea is top of the list of rock plants. Although 'no physical exercise is as useful and satisfactory as gardening in one's own garden', all the same advice was offered showing 'drawings that can be put into practice by your own personnel'. Advice by correspondence was also possible. With the help of data regarding size, wind and soil and the preferred flowering month, Moerheim produced a made-to-measure border design. In 1932 the tone was more modest. 'These are hard times, do not neglect your garden!' The catalogues were illustrated with letters from enthusiastic clients. Shipments in excess of 10 guilders were delivered free at station.

63

Moerheim Catalogue (1930)

64

Public Works Department Amsterdam   the Amsterdam Woods (1931-1937)

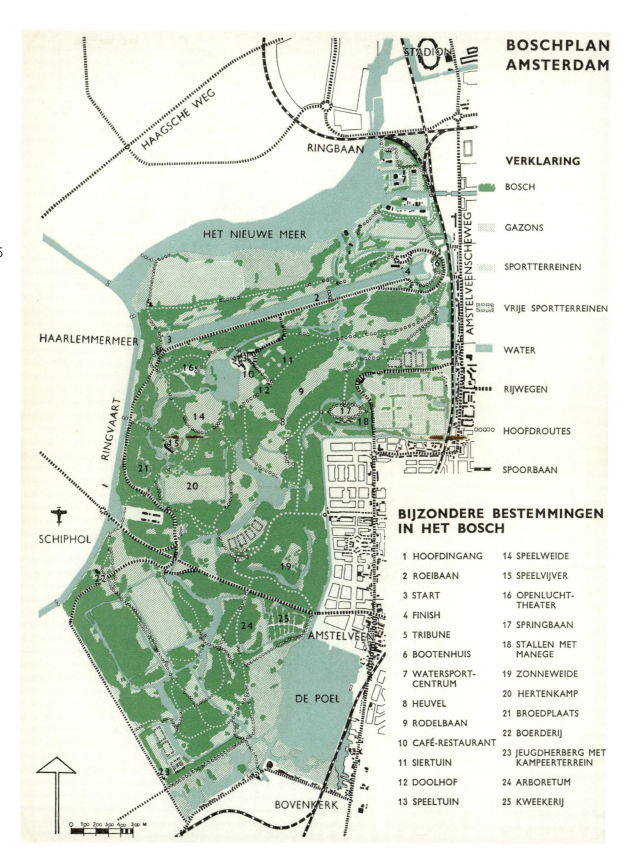

65

BOSCHPLAN AMSTERDAM

HAAGSCHE WEG

RINGBAAN

STADION

HET NIEUWE MEER

HAARLEMMERMEER

RINGVAART

SCHIPHOL

AMSTELVEENSCHEWEG

AMSTELVEEN

DE POEL

BOVENKERK

0 100 200 300 400 500 M

VERKLARING

- BOSCH
- GAZONS
- SPORTTERREINEN
- VRIJE SPORTTERREINEN
- WATER
- RIJWEGEN
- HOOFDROUTES
- SPOORBAAN

BIJZONDERE BESTEMMINGEN IN HET BOSCH

1 HOOFDINGANG
2 ROEIBAAN
3 START
4 FINISH
5 TRIBUNE
6 BOOTENHUIS
7 WATERSPORT-CENTRUM
8 HEUVEL
9 RODELBAAN
10 CAFÉ-RESTAURANT
11 SIERTUIN
12 DOOLHOF
13 SPEELTUIN
14 SPEELWEIDE
15 SPEELVIJVER
16 OPENLUCHT-THEATER
17 SPRINGBAAN
18 STALLEN MET MANEGE
19 ZONNEWEIDE
20 HERTENKAMP
21 BROEDPLAATS
22 BOERDERIJ
23 JEUGDHERBERG MET KAMPEERTERREIN
24 ARBORETUM
25 KWEEKERIJ

Public Works Department Amsterdam the Amsterdam Woods (1931-1937)

C. van den Heuvel   garden villa, Eindhoven

G. Bleeker   garden, Aerdenhout (1930)

M. Ruys garden with artificial pond, 't Gooi

M. Ruys garden of country house De Vennen, Harenermolen

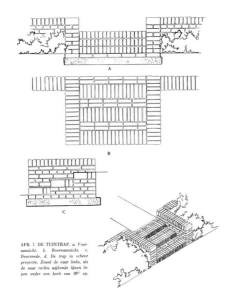

AFB. 7. DE TUINTRAP. *a. Voor-
aanzicht. b. Bovenaanzicht. c.
Doorsnede. d. De trap in scheve
projectie. Zowel de naar links, als
de naar rechts wijkende lijnen lo-
pen onder een hoek van 30° op.*

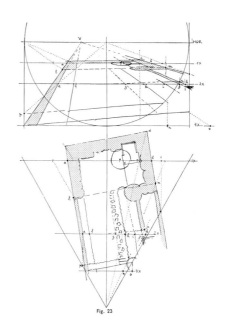

Fig. 23

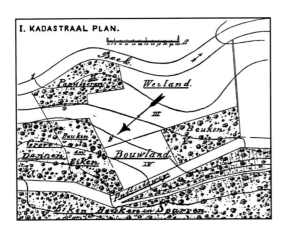

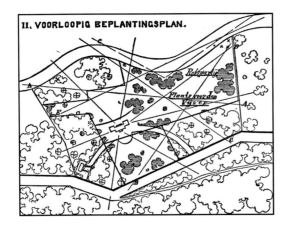

G. Bleeker garden, Overveen (1930)

J.T.P. Bijhouwer perspective construction, an indispensable aid from the pre-computer era

H.F. Hartogh Heys van Zouteveen four sketches planting for large residential area

Tulips planted in beds along established patterns

The popular rock garden in its final design by **H. Copijn**

Brinkman and Van der Vlugt garden at Sonneveld House, Rotterdam (1932)

G. Bleeker open-air theatre, Vierhouten near Nunspeet (1924-1935)

W.M. Dudok Town Hall, Hilversum (1924-1931)

H.P. Berlage Municipal Museum, The Hague (1927-1935)

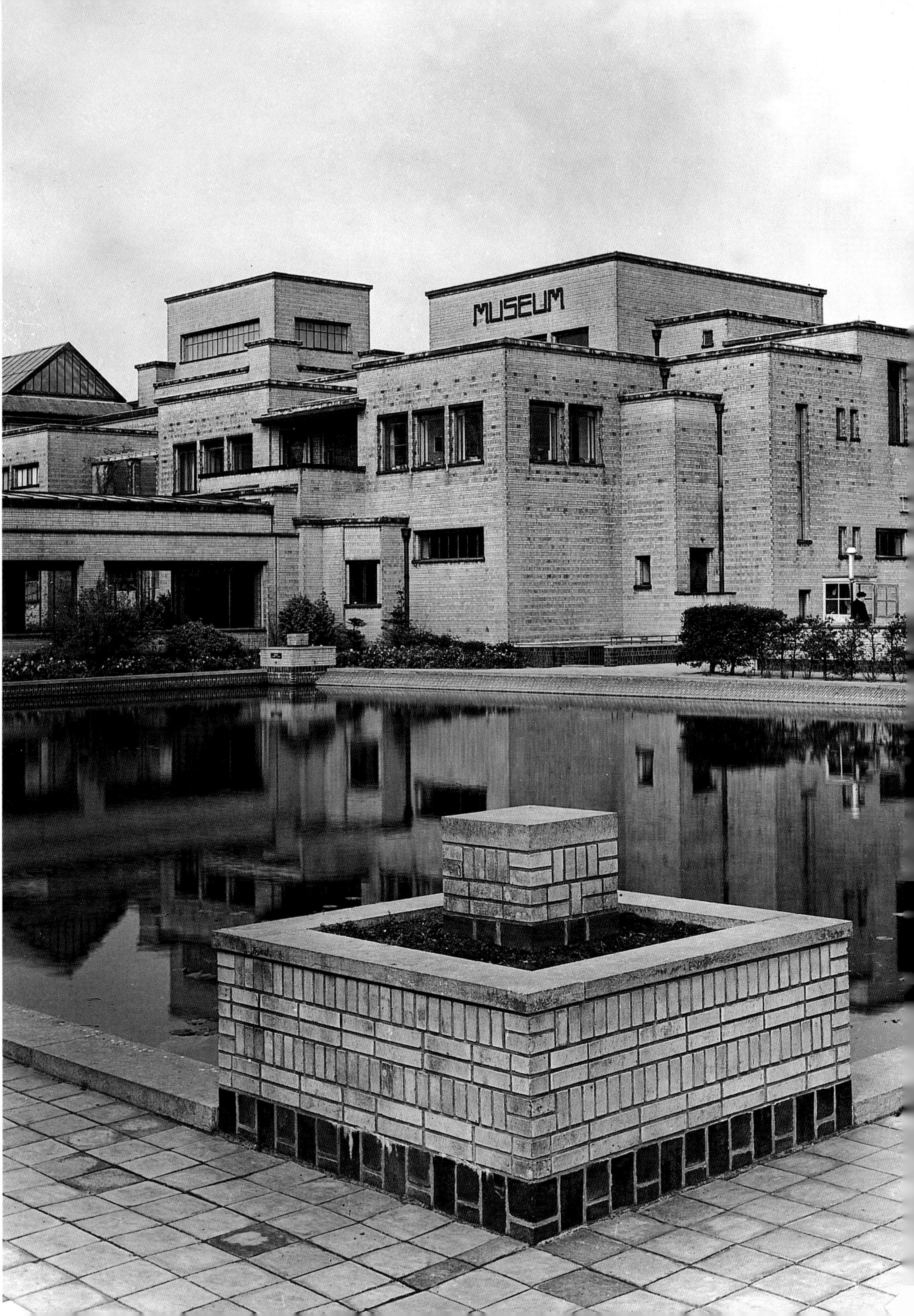

H.P. Berlage Municipal Museum, The Hague (1927-1935)

74

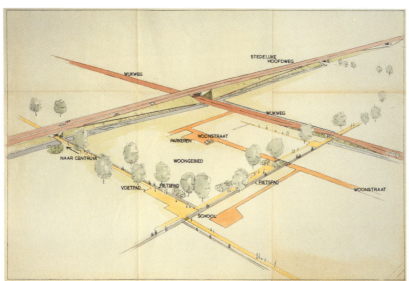

C. van Eesteren   garden suburbs, Amsterdam-West (1930)

C. van Eesteren   garden suburbs, Amsterdam-West – town planning analysis road system structure (1930)

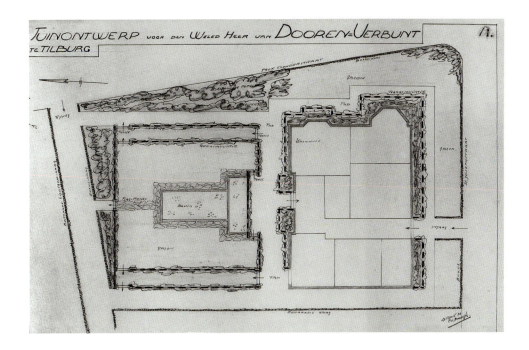

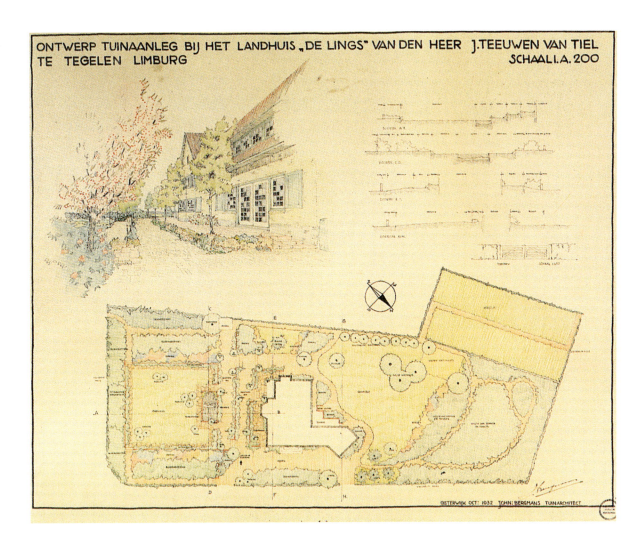

J. Bergmans   garden at villa of Mr Van Dooren-Verbunt (1930)

J. Bergmans   garden at country house De Lings of Mr J. Teeuwen van Tiel, Tegelen (1932)

Cover magazine 'Wegen' [Roads]

The provincial road from Soestdijk to Bilthoven

Much space reserved for cars in the garden design of **H. Roeters van Lennep**, Agnetapark – the pines, Delft (1931)

The beautiful Middachter Allee

• Reflection in wartime • redevelopment of Walcheren
• Heempark Amstelveen • Bleeker: a path is a necessary evil • Bordeaux mixture against leaf shedding
disease • gardening with your senses • good sense in
gardening • gardening by intuition • a nap during neap
tide • borders, how to make and maintain them

Reflection in wartime

During the war the green philosophy evolved
normally. The study group Cultural Landscapes
of the Contact Committee for Nature Conservation was founded for the purpose of making
plans for the post-war period. Nature conservation was seen as a matter not only of protecting
existing nature reserves, but also of cultural
scenery that was considered valuable. Members
were the biologist Victor Westhoff and the landscape architect J.T.P. Bijhouwer. Rather unex-
pectedly the ANWB also played a part as it provided accommodation to the science and the
public relations departments of the study group.
The committee's objective was to gain an insight
in the future of the entire landscape policy. In
addition, Westhoff also defined the policy of
the Dutch Young People's Association for Nature
Study. In the opinion of the members, 'real nature'
could be found outside the existing country
estates, in uncultivated territory. Westhoff set
against this that 'only man-managed landscapes
exist in the Netherlands. Therefore nature is
determined by culture. The fact that there is differentiation in development is only favourable
for specific flora and fauna. Nature conservation is wonderful, but far more complicated than
just maintaining threatened forests, sand drifts
and other special phenomena.' He struck a different note that made a lasting impression.

Redevelopment of Walcheren

The redevelopment of Walcheren was a pioneering effort in the field of landscaping. Towards
the end of the Second World War the island was
inundated and bombed. When reconstruction
was started, it was felt this was the opportunity
of a lifetime to realize a totally new redevelopment of the old cultural landscape.

J. Heimans wrote: 'The struggle to develop
a zoning scheme for an area that is not yet fully
utilized, is usually waged on three fronts simul-
taneously, namely those of the interests of farming, recreation and science. (…) In addition,
there are "roads" and "structures". In our civilized society, the struggle for precedence in this
interplay of forces is not labelled as "struggling",
but as "weighing up the interests involved".'

Where earlier the allocation of land had
mainly been based on expanding agricultural
parcels, now town planning, industry, and, cau-
tiously, recreation were included in the planning.
For such an extensive package of conditions
many experts were consulted. This resulted in
a plan in which the demands of farmers did not
lead to the biggest possible straight parcels.
The wish to reinstate the former 'Garden of
Zeeland', at least in part, also played an important role. Wide avenues were created in a scenic landscape. Parcels no longer needed to be
straight and square, but could also be irregular.
Old estates kept their original shape, whenever
possible. The loss of trees was compensated
again by planting on properties. Bijhouwer advocated planting typical of the region. He set forth
his ideas in his booklet Nederlandse Boerenerven
[Dutch Farmyards], published in the Heemschut
series in 1943.

The conclusion in the redevelopment of
Walcheren was that the old landscape was no
longer functional for reasons of economy and
the new landscape offered better prospects
for both farming and recreation. An optimistic,
post-war point of view. It was not possible to
afford the maintenance of hawthorn hedges or

the protection of rare vegetation. In the reconstruction phase of the post-war Netherlands the vital necessity was to keep the pot boiling.

Heempark in Amstelveen

In Amstelveen the Jac. P. Thijsse Park was developed in stages. This park was an extension of the Amsterdam Woods and was developed in accordance with the ideas Thijsse had put into practice in Thijsse's Garden in Bloemendaal from as early as 1925. There an oasis had been created where nature could go its own way in a controlled manner. Groups of plants keep each other, and the fauna as well, in balance.

The founder set great store by its educational aspect. Fifteen years later, an admirer of his, C.P. Broerse, dedicated the Heempark to Thijsse, the founder of nature conservation in the Netherlands. The peaty soil in Amstelveen is eminently suitable for indigenous forest and water plants. The park has its own nursery for self-sown plants which serves as a supplier to other parks and public gardens.

A path is a necessary evil

Country estates are the best examples to show how over the centuries landscapes were formed; they can be a true patchwork of gardening styles. Huis te Manpad in Heemstede certainly falls in this category. It is still associated with the well-known van Lennep family and in the meantime has become a protected estate. The range of designers who drafted plans that could be called products of their times, includes G. Bleeker. The combination of meandering forest paths and slightly classic garden plants near the house was completely reorganized by him. He was also the landscaping advisor to the Heemstede local council. Bleeker liked to work in different styles. He held strong views on the size of the garden in relation to its layout. His still strong aversion to paths, which actually dated back to his 'Springer' period, is remarkable. Meanwhile, paths have been upgraded again with the 'modern landscapers', even to the extent of becoming a supporting element

in the garden layout. But Bleeker's heart was not in it, for: 'A path is a necessary evil and one should not plan too many of them, as they disturb the quiet atmosphere.'

Harvesting from one's own garden

In 1940 the shape and the function of a garden were closely related. Gardening was a widespread hobby and there was a great need of, mostly practical, knowledge. Books appeared that try to tell readers everything about a gar-den in one book. For instance, the sub-title of C. Kromdijk's book Onze Tuin [Our Garden] is Bloemen, vruchten en groenten uit eigen tuin [Flowers, Fruits and Vegetables from Your Own Garden]. In the introduction the job of a garden architect is discussed: 'This job cannot be learned in a short course; it really cannot be learned at all, for you need to possess the gift, the talent to be able to create something artistic.' In the initial stages a flower, vegetable and/or fruit garden is the basis. A garden yielding useful products is still very popular. The technical side is highlighted – instructions how to use Bordeaux mixture to fight leaf shedding disease in berries – and many casual tips concerning shape are given. A long citation: 'Wherever one lays out a garden, the surroundings will always have to be taken into account. In town gardens we usually face walls or fences; not a very nice view and therefore we like to hide such objects as much as possible by planting evergreens. Camouflaging of the borders not only yields a better looking garden, but the area also looks much bigger. When we build a detached villa, we will have to consider the surrounding scenery; to arrive at a harmonious whole the garden should match the surroundings as much as possible.' Many of these recommendations are fairly compelling. 'Paths should on no account be too wide and should be slightly mossy, and they should never be straight.' Or: 'Grass between broom and heather is out of place.' As in most books from that period it is a passionate plea for a rock garden and a recommendation to use exotic evergreen conifers to do up the garden in winter.

Useful gardening

In the years after the Second World War the architect P. Verhagen wrote a book on gardening, called Het geluk van den tuin [The Bliss of the Garden]; for many years it was the bible of hortiphilics.

In hiding in his sister's house, he committed all his memories of gardens and plants to paper. He did not see gardening 'as filling in leisure time', but 'as a beautiful and meaningful link between man and nature, whereby man should comply with nature as much as possible with loving abandon.' Verhagen analysed the garden and the gardener and placed them in a historic framework. He described the birth of the garden from the days of the nomads. The author started with the settling of man in a fixed place where he tilled his own plot inside a fence. A requirement was that the garden and the man tilling the soil were in balance. 'For as long as we lose the thread of our rightful desires in our garden, we will fail to achieve anything in our green spaces.' The concept of the 'Nieuwe Bouwers' [New Builders] – the garden being an extension of the house – was considered a first class error by the author. 'You cannot turn the house inside out without affecting its nature. The house is there for you not to be outside. In our houses we seek protection from nature and its squalls, in the garden we welcome nature and try to put it in the right mood. So, by all means let us keep this contrast, even cultivate it and give any mingling a wide berth.' What is the gardener's job? 'To create a steady or at least a less fleeting entity out of the transient growing and flowering of plants, giving his garden a character of its own by pulling together all welcome elements.'

Gardening with your senses

All aspects of handling nature can be found in Het geluk van den tuin [The Bliss of the Garden]. Sensory, empirical gardening is interspersed with attempts to define. What exactly is a cultural landscape? The landscape which is born when man intervenes and changes nature to satisfy his own needs. The difference between a garden and a park is concentrated on the visitor. In the park visitors are entertained; they should have a good time. Action, rest, bustle and peace and quiet according to their needs. In the garden it is a matter of combined play between nature and the gardener. Here he can give free rein to his urge to shape things. For a nature lover is not necessarily a good gardener. The author professes to be both, but never at the same time. In his capacity of author of books that are constructive as to content and therefore rare, Verhagen breaks a lance for keeping eyes, ears and, in particular, the nose wide open. 'This drives me to encourage you to concentrate on smelling, for the sense of smell is the most difficult sense to control. The smell activates our memories and so links today's enjoyment to that of earlier years or even a long time ago. This could be the smell of tar on a shed or fence or the smell of old manure on farmland in spring. As it is, you are hardly ever without some indefinable smell wafting through the garden, something you are hardly conscious of but still experience. The smell of the salty beach or the sea, penetrating far beyond the dunes, may even leave a salty taste on your lips; the moist smell of the foggy dew or of a morning mist in late summer, or the smell of smoke from a wood-fired fireplace precipitated in misty weather, or the smell of ozone after a thunderstorm. And, does the smell of hay resemble the fragrance of flowers?'

Gardening by intuition

Gardening books in the forties offered many compelling recommendations. Green 'compartmentalization' pervaded all gardens. Captions in books told you what was right and what was wrong. Every social class stuck to the expression of verdure meant for it and imposed from above. Every innovation was strongly opposed to the existing garden layouts. Here, too, Verhagen disagreed. A gardener should follow his own feelings as much as possible. 'Plant your garden the way you like it best', is one of his creeds. From the sheer admiration of everything that is perceived in the garden, a natural sense of design regarding the choice of plants and layout arises. The call for a little anarchy was a unique statement in a gardening book from an era in which gardening ranked low on the list of priorities. Everything breathes a relaxed atmosphere. A contemporary garden guru, Christopher Lloyd, once answered the umpteenth well-intended question from a visitor, what was the best time to sow a certain plant or top prune a specific rose. He said this was different for everybody. 'I myself do it when I feel like it. And, if I am lucky, the sun shines to warm my back.' This is in sharp contrast with the pre-selected, ready-to-plant borders already laid out by Mien Ruys.

A nap during neap tide

With Verhagen, the man who later inspired Louis le Roy, everything boiled down to experience. All factors were crucial. 'A rainy day always seems much wetter to the people sitting at home than to the persevering walker.' If you have not felt all seasons on your skin and cannot name all moments in a day, your sense of gardening grows poorer. 'A day is not really a good day, if you have not woken up at dawn and enjoyed the beginning of that day. Not when the sun is rising, but at daybreak; that experience will stay with you throughout the day. The brightest summer day will not consume the memory of that hesitant, tentative awakening of daylight. It is at its most beautiful on quiet days in late summer, when hazy early-morning veils shelter the heavy dew from the sunlight and the humid morning mist may often stay until noon. Occasionally the morning may gently change into a splendid evening, without the intervening afternoon. This is no great loss, for it always is a bit of 'neap tide'. Then everything seems to come to a standstill, as if nature takes a nap. In any case, at least in summer, this is the least exciting time of day.

Moerheim Gardening Catalogues 1939 and 1940

Moerheim's 1939 catalogue opened with full-page black-and-white photographs showing gardens designed by Moerheim. It showed spacious lawns, flagstone paths and all this fringed with flowery borders. In the catalogue attention was paid to eight new varieties of roses, ferns, climbers, fruit trees and shrubs. A fresh page with evergreen hedges and edges gave a survey of boxwood and yew. Many black-and-white photographs showed plants such as iris and meconopsis. In the year of the war, 1940, a simplified version of the catalogue was issued. 'A well laid-out garden is the only thing to provide joy and compensation for everything we have to do without.' It was not only the war that prompted austerity. The publishing house Kosmos offered: Borders, hoe men ze maakt en onderhoudt [Borders, How to Make and Maintain Them], by Mien Ruys. And for the lazy ones among its clients there was a package Collection A, in which 75 plants in 25 varieties could be found, at 13.50 guilders.

Moerheim Catalogue (1940)

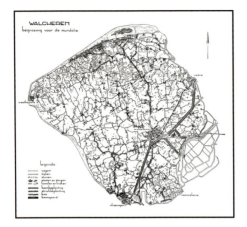

82

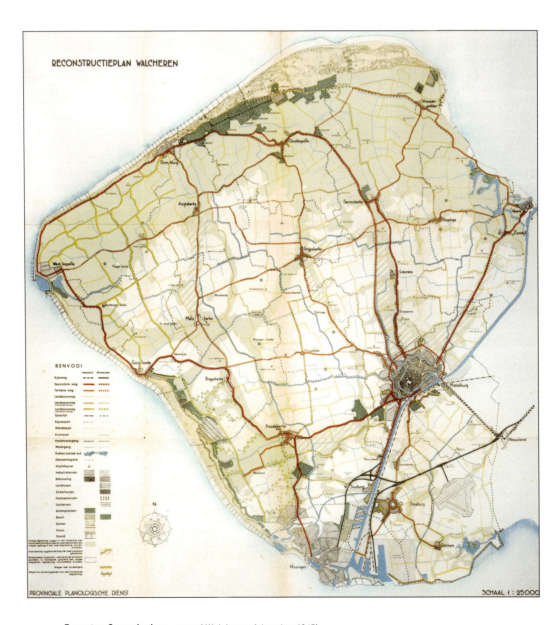

Forestry Commission   map of Walcheren (situation 1947)

Forestry Commission   map of Walcheren – future planting (1947)

R.J. Benthem, N.M. de Jonge   plan for new layout of Walcheren (1946)

C.P. Broerse Jac.P. Thijsse Park, Amstelveen (1940, 1949)

84

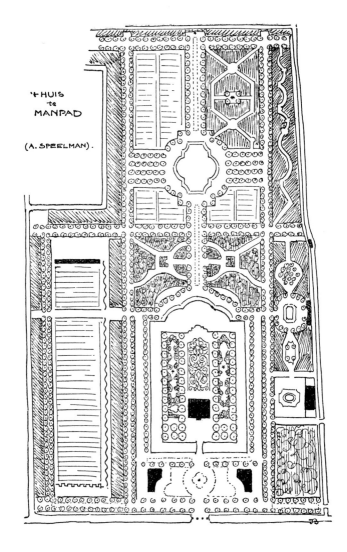

'tHUIS
te
MANPAD

(A. SPEELMAN).

G. Bleeker Huis te Manpad (1946)

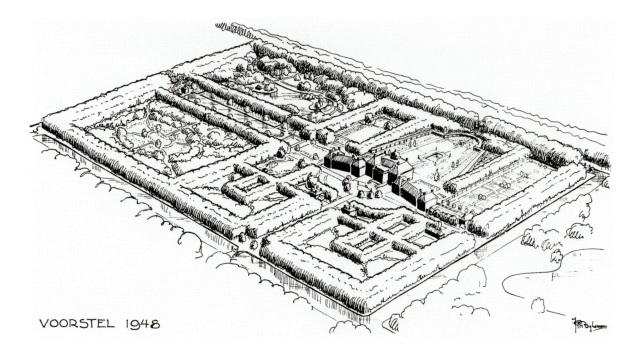

VOORSTEL 1948

E. Ilseman water colour of the rock garden in Twickel: 'the baroness's little garden' (1942)

J.T.P. Bijhouwer Huis ten Bosch, The Hague (proposal 1948)

Motorways

Temporary allotment gardens in enclosed garden Witte de Withstraat, Amsterdam (1942)

88

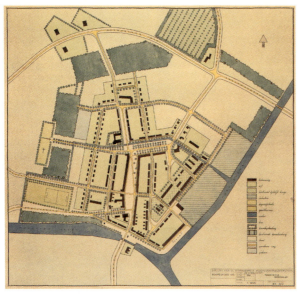

J.T.P. Bijhouwer   planting schedule Noordoostpolder (1944)

IJsselmeerpolders Department   plan for the village of Marknesse (1947)

Noordoostpolder (situation 1995)

• A plea for diversity • green fairy-tales in De Efteling
• flower bulbs in the Keukenhof • studying in green
areas • green windbreaks in the polder • Texel as an
experiment • land consolidation in the Tielerwaard
• distinction between garden and landscape • factory
and row building sites

Clear and modern

In the post-war years everything had to be
built up from scratch. The recommendations
suggested by Elly Buwalda in her book De Tuin
[The Garden] are based on bare land. First,
protection against the wind was needed – 'an
authentic coppice is ideal, but a stone wall
will also do' – before a garden can thrive in the
lee. Photographic material arrived from abroad,
since the new Dutch gardens laid out after 1945
were still too immature and could only be shown
in perspective drawings. Moreover, the views
on gardens had been influenced by international
concepts. The Scandinavian influence on interior design was extended to the garden. In her
advice for garden layout the author discarded
the pre-war patronizing tone by a fresh approach,
this is allowed and that is not allowed. She took
the uniform character of Dutch gardens in 1950
as her starting point for a clean-up operation.
'Everywhere you find the same standard gardens,
usually with vague curved lines, meaningless
walls, lawns that are too small, miles of privet
hedges, not to mention the tasteless rock gardens laid out with large chunks of cinder.' So,
what is the solution? 'Try and keep a sense of
moderation, do not demand things not fitting
the size of your yard. Do not mess about on a
small scale; it will only make your garden look
untidy and restless.' She also offers advice on
architecture: always colour, always a green and
natural environment. Later chapters contain
detailed recommendations including technical
progress in garden aids. Motor mowers, hedge-
trimmers and automatic sprinklers became
available to the smaller town gardens as well.

The glory of allotment gardens

Not everyone enjoyed the privilege of a house
with a garden. Allotment gardens were the
solution. Originally, the allotment garden concept was rooted in the belief that air and light
would uplift the worker and his family. In the
fifties this belief was a thing of the past. During
the war the allotment garden was the main
greengrocer. Besides, however, the allotment
gar-dens gradually developed into pocket-sized
recreational parks. Next to the railway lines
in the Netherlands there were unused plots
made available to the personnel by the Dutch
Railways management so they can grow their
own vegetables, or flowers to adorn their front
room. The allotment gardens turned into a true
culture, where social contacts and social control were very much present. Everything was
done in a team, from chores such as weeding
the paths to carnival parties in the canteen.
So, in the middle of the twentieth century the
garden provided vegetables and gladiolas and
dahlias were lined up in the kitchen garden.
Only afterwards the garden began to follow
the gardeners' prosperity.

A fairy-tale in De Efteling

'Do you have difficulty walking, this little
house is not for stalking.' Generations of Dutch
people grew up with Anton Pieck's drawings.
A modern manufacturer of electric light bulbs
used his drawings on birthday calendars to sell
the romantic creamy light of their bulbs. The
same company, Philips, was the first to intro-
duce the concept of a fairy-tale park in Noord-
Brabant. Its success made the mayor of Kaatsheuvel take the decision to create a fairy-tale
park in the dunes near Drunen. Now Snowwhite

lies under the firs and the 'try-your-strength-machine' towers above everything. In 1952 the notion of an amusement park was still very novel: a playground, sports fields and ten fairy tales. The Nature Park De Efteling Foundation wished to promote tourism, 'largely in the Roman Catholic spirit'. Arms should not be too bare and a two-piece bathing suit was out of the question. Right from the start there were a million visitors per year! In 1954 the pedal trains for children were added and in 1958 the magic carpet started flying. The park as we know it today, complete with Pythons and Piranhas, dates from a later period. Initially the fairy tales were the big attraction, as were the facilities round them. The toilets were signposted with signs reading 'Do number two' and the waste bin is called 'Fatso'; he shouts 'Paper here' and says 'Thank you', when the paper actually lands in the bin. In 1966 the fairy-tale wood was expanded with The Water Lilies and queen Fabiola's frogs until the time arrived when fairy tales were no longer 'in' and the public demanded more exiting attractions such as roller coasters, big dippers and white-water canoeing. When the park was expanded there also was an increasing need to adapt the original pinewood, by introducing park-like measures following the spirit of the times. As a result the rock gardens appeared in Kaatsheuvel. Open space planning is managed privately.

Flower bulbs in the Keukenhof

A different type of entertainment was created in Lisse, in the heart of the bulb-growing area. The house, the Keukenhof, was vacant after billeting during the Second World War and did not really serve any purpose. The appearance of the estate was fairly predictable: a park, arranged in landscape style by Zocher, Jr. and his son Louis. A forest was planted, ponds were dug and even an oriental touch was added with bamboo, rhododendrons and fuchsias. On 1 January 1949 mayor Lambooij happened to be at the Keukenhof to attend a fire drill. He then spoke the historic words: 'This would be an ideal spot for an open-air exhibition of bulbous flowers.' So the idea to build this park, that was to meet with worldwide acclaim, was born. Later, the castle and the adjacent surroundings were too become a bird sanctuary. The flowers, admired by millions of tourists, occupy a relatively small part of the dune estate. The manner of exhibiting the flowers betrays a natural development. In the beginning especially top-class flowers such as tulips, daffodils and hyacinths could be seen covering large areas, but later more variety was introduced. Special bulbous plants were given a place of their own and the exhibition period was extended. Indoor exhibitions and welcoming visitors in the evenings helped to increase the attractiveness. Outside the Keukenhof the bulb fields are there for everyone to see free of charge. According to some foreign garden architects this is the biggest land-art park in the Netherlands. Without the benefit of a designer the greatest spring colour festival was created in the Dutch dune district.

Studying in green areas

One of the optimist ideas from the post-war period was that studying in a green environment yields better results; all elements of students' life, being close together under the trees, present a positive world view. In Enschede, such a concentration after the American example is practised. The campus of Twente University has university buildings, housing units for students and professors, but also a refectory, a library and a building housing a lunch-theatre called 'Culture-Sandwich'. The first designs were based on the New Realism. The architects van de Broek and Bakema designed buildings between austere lawns and scattered groups of trees. In the following decades different ideas were developed and between the trees houses appeared; in 1967 Piet Blom built a restaurant, La Bastille, as a meeting place. The concentration concept and the view on efficiency were clear and on paper it seemed to fit perfectly. However, young students wanted to do more than just look outside and watch rabbits frolicking in the fields, far away from the pubs in the city centre. Besides, a labyrinth serving as a refectory is far from practical. Fortunately, they can follow their noses and find a restaurant.

Green windbreaks in the polder

The planning of the Wieringermeer still bore the hallmark of traditional notions about living and working. On the other hand, landscaping experts opposed this and suggested that the next polder, the Noordoostpolder, should be the ideal place to represent the new social concepts and the resulting society. After many years of discussion and conferences De 8 architects were finally allowed to put their ideas into practice. In the Noordoostpolder the village Nagele was designed by some thirty architects – who were to become quite famous later – in accordance with the principles of the New Realism. Light, air, straight lines and space were the main ideas on which De 8 architects based themselves. Mien Ruys, W. Boer and J.T.P. Bijhouwer made the layout for the green spaces and a planting scheme. In plain words, the design boiled down to a large angular circle, with a green central area, where the school, the church and the town hall were situated. Round them residential areas were built in the style of Modern Building. 'Nagele has a patent on the flat roof.'

The green areas and the street plan were executed in a squared pattern. The residential areas were constructed in accordance with sketches by Rietveld. Workers, middle class and prominent citizens all live in the same village, but the differences in social class have been expressed in the architecture and the filling-in of the gardens. The 'lower' one's position on the social scale, the smaller the front garden, and the package of perennials supplied. Canals meander through the compact village at right angles and run off into the distance in straight lines. Round the village there is a protective ring of indigenous trees forming a recreational area. This is no luxury in this flat, bare and new land. The trees form a windbreak and are ideal for a walk in the woods.

Texel as an experiment

According to Bijhouwer, who is an expert on Dutch landscapes, the flat countryside in the Netherlands offers a great variety in landscapes. Any changes implemented in the existing scenery should be supervised with the utmost care. All the same he maintains not all old reclamations should be protected without question. If such developments have outlived their usefulness, they should be redeveloped. This sort of statement impressed the Ministry of Agriculture so much, that a landscaping expert was appointed to sit on the land consolidation committee of Texel. Land surveyor R.J. Benthem, an advisor to the Dutch Forestry Commission, saw the advantages of agricultural modernization and stood up for the preservation of cores of dikes and open structures. In addition, the requirements of expanding recreation were incorporated into a new vision. Land consolidation was renamed regrouping of land. The open and closed character of built-up areas was taken seriously. A new road would be constructed as a winding road, following the course of the river. Trees were planted alternately on the right and the left side of the road, to provide some variety for cyclists and walkers. Sunken roads and belt planting were given the same serious consideration as streamlined water management and the larger, rectangular agricultural plots.

Distinction between garden and landscape

In the post-war years there was a strong need for a fresh understanding of concepts, the circumstances having changed considerably. The new Land Consolidation Act of 1954 put the task of regrouping on the shoulders of Forestry Commission engineers, whose first priority was efficiency. In the short term the straight, strict solutions were ideal for the agricultural sector. What exactly were these changes? Large, square plots, easy to work for new farm machinery, straight drainage channels complete with weirs and barbed wire instead of hawthorn hedges as fences. The Dutch Garden Architects Association

(BNT) launches a fierce attack against this state monopoly; they felt shunted off from such a massive regrouping of plots. The government, in its turn, feared possible 'artistic visions on re-allocated parcels of land'. Garden architects, it was felt, have a tendency to suggest rather exotic varieties of plants to embellish roads. This clashed with the prevailing desire to choose easy planting methods.' 'On the other hand, landscape architects feel the need to distinguish themselves from garden designers. Bijhouwer defined it as follows: 'Landscape architecture means creating a satisfactory and habitable landscape, using plants on a limited scale, in areas mainly consisting of fields already earmarked for production. On the other hand the garden', so Bijhouwer continues, 'is a place to be used to one's satisfaction without any commercial purpose'. Clear Dutch definitions in the fifties with their land division and compartmentalization. The consequences of the first land consolidations only became apparent in the following years. Single-crop farming resulted in decimation of flora and fauna. Drainage was a problem. The groundwater level dropped to a dangerous level. Beautiful scenery was also hard to find after land consolidation.

Land consolidation in the Tielerwaard, Modernization blew through the traditional agricultural areas like a punishing wind. The relatively isolated position of the Betuwe quickly came to an end after 1958. There was an urge to adapt the planning of the agricultural area round Tiel to the demands of our modern times. Old plots were extended and given a different function. Due to lack of funds not everything could be rebuilt from scratch. The old earth walls, canals and dikes were retained, but this was largely because of budgetary considerations. New provincial roads halved travelling times and for heavy traffic to and from the brickyards special roads were built. Dikes could be strengthened, because houses on the dikes could simply be expropriated under the Urban Renewal Act. New areas came into existence

with their own contemporary infrastructure. Roadside planting was combined with the remaining plants and watercourses. Ten years later motorways crossed each other at the Deil interchange and opened up all horizons. Untidy standard tree orchards, that were difficult to run, were replaced by straight lines of bush fruit trees, which were easier to manage, more efficient and more profitable. The same applied to houses, barns and farms. Modern times demanded modernized management. People chose new houses, concentrated on a central axis, if possible in a design typical of the region. In the seventies city dwellers, who loved to live in the peaceful green Tielerwaard, discovered second homes in the Betuwe. They can go for a swim in a sand pit in the Linge Woods, already quite mature-looking in the eighties. Within a short period age-old structures were altered beyond all recognition.

Plant Breeders' Catalogues 1950 and 1954

In 1950 the Moerheim catalogue became increasingly simple. For pictures of flowers it referred to the Vasteplantenboek [Perennials Book] by Mien Ruys and for trees and shrubs to the Flora der Cultuurgewassen in Nederland [Flora of Cultivated Plants in the Netherlands], a standard work by the expert B.K. Boom. The Rozenjaarboek [Yearbook of Roses] could be ordered from a publishing house set up by Moerheim. Architectural design concentrated in particular on the repair of war damage to gardens. There was plenty of work as was evident from the notification that requests for designs would be dealt with in the order in which they came in. The catalogue listed many 'big' products: ornamental and avenue trees, hedges and borders, azaleas, conifers and rock plants. And, of course, the delphinium moerheimi, completely white. In 1954 the catalogue showed ready-to-use garden designs, A, B and C, intended for private gardens. In addition, designs for 'planting near house-building and row building' were recommended. Offices and factories were addressed as well. 'For the benefit of personnel, factory sites were provided with spacious canteens surrounded by colourful flower gardens.' Of course, strong plants requiring little maintenance were planted.

Moerheim Catalogue (1950)

The running-wild garden in **M. Ruys**' experimental gardens Moerheim, Dedemsvaart (1954)

Motorway number 2

W. van der Lee flower exhibition Keukenhof, Lisse (1949)

A. Pieck   amusement park De Efteling, Kaatsheuvel (1951, situation 1993)

98

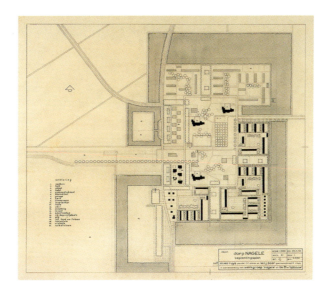

99

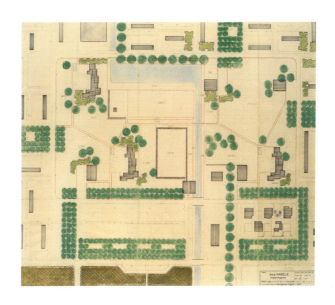

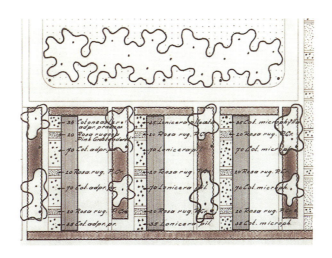

W.C.J. Boer, M. Ruys, J.T.P. Bijhouwer planting scheme, Nagele (1953)

W.C.J. Boer, M. Ruys, J.T.P. Bijhouwer planting scheme, Nagele (1953)

W.C.J. Boer, M. Ruys, J.T.P. Bijhouwer detailed planting scheme, Nagele (1953)

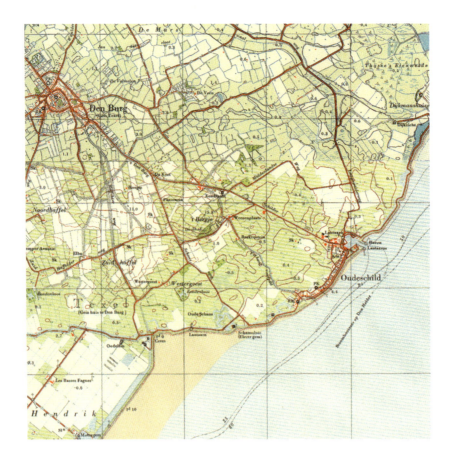

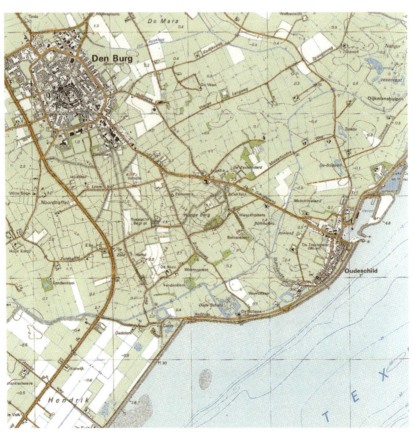

Forestry Commission landscaping plan Texel (1953)

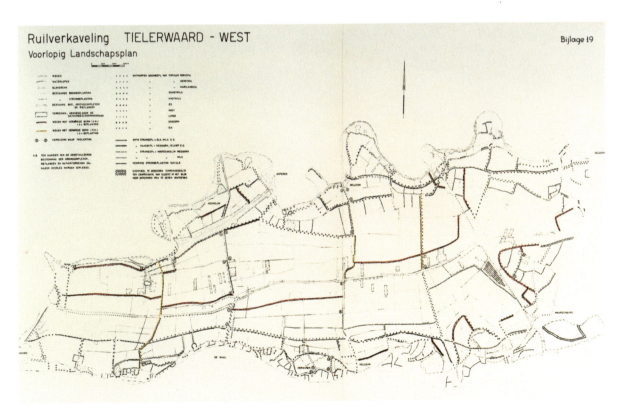

Forestry Commission landscaping plan for the Tielerwaard-West, land consolidation, construction A15, recreation pond (1958)

TEHUIS VOOR BEJAARDEN
GORREDIJK

J.T.P. Bijhouwer scale-model statue garden, Kröller-Müller Museum, National Park De Hoge Veluwe (1955)

J. Vroom garden old people's home, Gorredijk (1954)

C. van Empelen model garden flora (1953)

104

M. Ruys, J.T.P. Bijhouwer atmospheric examples of gardens for residences, enclosed inner courtyards in village

or town communities or in town districts with many children (situation 1950-1960)

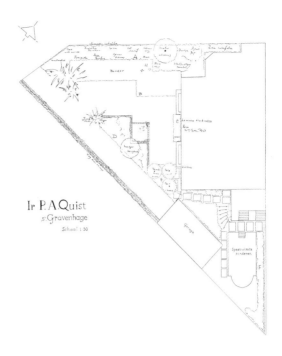

Ir P.A.Quist
s'Gravenhage
Schaal 1:50

P. Daniëls garden design for Mr P.A. Quist, The Hague (1958)

W.C.J. de Boer Gijsbrecht van Aemstelpark (1959, situation 1985)

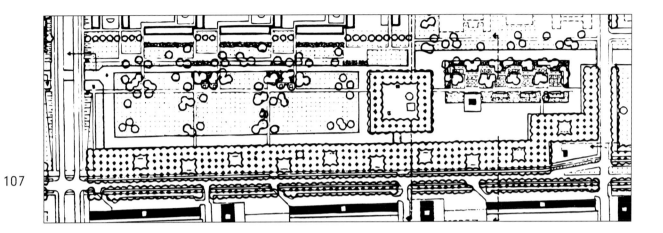

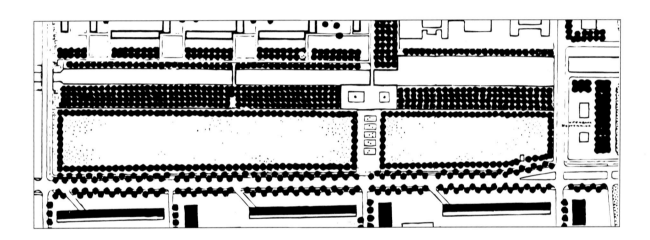

W.C.J. de Boer prize contest design for Gijsbrecht van Aemstelpark (1959)

H. Warnau prize contest design for Gijsbrecht van Aemstelpark (1959)

W.C.J. de Boer Gijsbrecht van Aemstelpark (1959, situation 1970)

1960-1970

• Leave nature to its own devices • a residential area in a green environment • tension between near and far • local and global designing • vista park by Warnau and Boer • beauty in the consolidated 'Polder van Altena' • Mien Ruys and J.T.P. Bijhouwer reassess awareness of nature • as warm as ripe corn

Louis le Roy

Nature as an easing-off agent. Nature can be left to its own devices without any human interference. Why should we pump away all the fresh water from the Netherlands and then desalinate salt water again? Louis le Roy asked himself the question: 'When will we finally wake up and stop dreaming of a manageable culture we can manipulate in an ever faster moving society?' Le Roy wanted an approach to nature in which nature will be left free to do what it is supposed to do. Aboveground and underground. This would bring the designer to a way of planning which encourages variety in particular. The incidence of light should be captured at several levels, bacteria must be allowed to carry on undisturbed for years on end, and low walls should have openings and not be closed. Surface water should be connected to the groundwater in order to stimulate logical vegetation. In fact, the mechanical interventions by man should be aimed at reinforcing the cycle of matter that has been with us for ages. 'More hard work is carried out more efficiently under the ground than above it.'

In 1966 Louis le Roy built the Kennedy Public Garden in Heerenveen in accordance with ecological principles. Human involvement was restricted to a minimum. In the seventies this created quite a bit of commotion in the world of Parks and Public Gardens Departments. It turned out to be a labour intensive job to protect spontaneous natural development. The crop protection chemical DDT was still available, although it was strictly forbidden later. Lawns should be close-cut and free of clover and dandelions. One-sided selection of plants would lead to unbalanced growth and plagues of insects. From the date he started his first public garden Le Roy conducted a true crusade against, as he put it, the pessimism of the seventies. In the eighties he surprised friend and foe with his 'eco-cathedral', a compound measuring 8 acres, where two thousand lorry loads of stones, rubble and sand were dumped, on and among which nature could develop as it pleased. The result was amazing. In this habitat butterflies flutter that used to be unique to the south of France. Once the walls became overgrown, new loads were dumped again. Frisians at the Frisian reunion all contributed a pebble or a stone. In the course of the years, public opinion changed from heavy scepticism to wild enthusiasm. The eco-cathedral is now managed by the Estafette Foundation whose aim it is to pass on the good work to the following generations. Le Roy received official prizes, and his points of view, extreme at the time, marked the start of a wide public debate. Examples can be found from the manor house garden in Baexum to the Blue Room in Wageningen. Louis le Roy returned to nature the space it needs to quietly carry on its business, in particular for the benefit of us, human beings, who, hopefully, will eventually be in less of a hurry.

Angerslo, living in a green environment

The inhabitants of Angerslo also live near to green areas in this suburb of Emmen in the province of Drenthe, a recent housing development designed by N. de Boer and A.J.M. de Jong with the usual terrace houses popular in the sixties. André de Jong listed the desires and wishes of the local population regarding housing and living conditions. He also took stock of striking elements in the existing landscape. Every wooded bank, special tree, ditch, canal and coppice was charted. 'If anyone wants a tree to be felled, he will have to explain to me why.' The newly built district was star-shaped and, where possible, the points 'penetrate' the woods. The outskirts reaches into the old town centre. The new road system was made up of a wide feeder road that branched off into a number of cul-de-sacs: the residential area with restrictions to slow down traffic is born. All round the houses nature is close by. Parking lots are partially paved so that grass may grow between the paved areas. Traffic flows are divided. Cyclists, pedestrians and drivers all have their own way through the woods. An underground feeder road to the shopping centre was constructed to divide the traffic flows, but later was felt to be rather creepy! The densely built-up centre is made up of local shops. From there, the building gradually becomes less dense towards the outlying districts and the original landscape. In its original design, Angerslo is the classic example for many other residential area with restrictions to slow down traffic. In Emmen concepts concerning the integration of town and country were worked out in detail in the districts Emmerhout and Rietlanden.

Flevopolder turned into a grand landscape

To a greater extent than was the case in the Wieringermeer and the Noordoostpolder, attention shifted to landscaping rather than agriculture in the Flevopolder. Landscape gardener N.M. de Jonge was the 'father' of the open space planning in the eastern part of Flevoland. 'Man does not function properly, until he is linked to his natural habitat, to soil, climate, plant and animal.' The strongest landscape is one that is richly differentiated. For that reason large parts of the new Flevopolders were turned into forests and nature reserves. The route of migratory birds helped to choose the right spots. Creating much open space outside was an important issue as well. 'One should not try and create scenic areas like those in the Achterhoek; the Achterhoek is a different kettle of fish.' Where

in the Noordoostpolder it was largely a matter of emulating the traditional polder landscape, in Flevoland the accents were to be provided by the panoramic view, the tension between 'here and there', and the clouds in the sky, without changing it into an uncultured desert. Not all the dead straight roads are lined with trees. The motorway that was built later, runs through the scenery without the benefit of trees and, near the Ketelbrug, it gives drivers the feeling of moving below sea level. Farms are isolated groups of buildings in the landscape. Farmers built their own buildings. For the first time feed silos appeared in the yards of the large plots. There was not only diversity in layout, but also in vegetation. This was a real bonus at a time when the need for recreation was growing. Large wooded and watery areas were created in Flevoland. There were only a few towns and villages in the new polder. The farms were bigger in size and because of mechanization fewer people worked on the farms. The centre of Lelystad was set up as a modern urban centre following a plan by C. van Eesteren. The centre of the village of Dronten was laid out with many grass strips, including sports fields, footpaths and a cemetery. In the event of expansion, part of the grass may disappear. The polders also became an overspill area for inhabitants of the older land and its growing population.

Local and global designing

After the Second World War houses were built first. Once a new neighbourhood had been more or less completed, the green spaces got a chance. This also happened in Amsterdam, where in accordance with the General Expansion Plan, drawn up by the underrated Cornelis van Eesteren, a whole range of parks and public gardens were created. In addition, existing parks in the old city were embellished with fresh plants. The experienced garden architect Egbert Mos was appointed head of Public Works in 1956. He expanded the Amsterdam Woods, designed the rose garden in the Vondelpark in a structuralistic honeycomb style, he renovated the

Westerpark and he adorned the new west part of Amsterdam with a new string of green pearls: the Sloterpark round the Sloterplas, the green belt Gerbrandypark and Eendrachtspark with their aquatic playgrounds ('play-ponds') and crocuses forming a map of the Netherlands, and, finally, the initial impetus to the Rembrandtpark. These are the green lungs of the metropolis, all these straight, spacious, open parks, partly inspired by the straight Dutch polder landscape. They were mostly designed in a business-like style and occasionally in a watered down landscaping style, sometimes called neo-romanticism. In that same period Mos was also engaged in the preparations for the Floriade, the exhibition showing the quality products produced by Dutch nurserymen. The Beatrixpark, designed by his colleague Jacoba Mulder, was adapted and the Artsenijhof, a garden containing medicinal plants, was added. More to the south the Amstelpark was laid out, to form a transition from an austere to a casual ambience. Partly still angular, and partly showing the shapes of natural beauty, the park accommodates an iris garden, a rhododendron valley and many exotic trees. After the Floriade exhibition in 1972, the park serves as a city park. Mos continued to make his knowledge available to the Floriade staged near the Gaasperplas in 1982. International contacts he made in the course of these activities, requested him to produce designs, from Vienna to Paramaribo.

Vista park by Warnau and Boer

Biographies of landscape gardeners and garden architects show that many of them started off as architects or horticulturists and during their entire working life developed into all-rounders in the field of landscaping. A typical example is the career of Hans Warnau. Warnau's career started in tropical horticulture. After the war he developed plans for the planting of farm-yard trees in Zeeland rising from its ashes. He was employed by the Town Development Department in Amsterdam and worked with van Eesteren and Aldo van Eyck. Later he became a partner in a design firm, landscaping advisor to the state authority for the IJsselmeerpolders and he taught at several educational establishments. Besides, he found the time to compete in contests, held by the Association of Dutch Garden Architects. When, in 1959, Hans Warnau drafted his entry for the Gysbrecht van Aemstelpark, the Nieuwe Bouwen movement in architecture was at its height. The new Amsterdam district of Buitenveldert was built up of blocks of flats standing at right angles, and strips of grass in between lent the district a sense of splendour. Plenty of open spaces, wide streets and rows of trees set the scene. The design for the park fitted in with the neighbouring plots with their large, square lawns, double rows of indigenous trees and a central square serving as a meeting place. Warnau's colleague, Wim Boer, designed a similar set-up with three isolated blocks and this won him the prize. After the park had been completed in 1962, opinions were divided. Colleagues considered it a new high in garden architecture; visitors saw the park as open and too orderly.

The beauty of Altena

The sixties were a revolutionary period in land consolidation, too. The inventory drawn up of old areas in the polders of Altena refer to them as 'unspoilt natural beauty'. Beside the usual plans to increase water management, rearrange farmland and plan new roads to open up the area, a new method was developed. On the basis of a wider perspective, the landscaping consultant Maas designed a combination of arable land, meadows and woods, attractive to flora and fauna, farmer and holiday-maker. Arable land not only functions as a means of production, but also as open space between the edges of recreational woods and fresh water streams.

Reassessing awareness of nature

In the publication Leven met groen [Living with Plants], two authoritative voices, namely Mien Ruys and J.T.P. Bijhouwer, presented a clear view on plants, inside and outside the fence.

Mien Ruys advocated the layout of green areas in new developments to fit the needs of the users. 'Damage to plants that were put in the wrong place to start with, should not be blamed on the destructive mania of the residents, but on human laziness, on people trying to find short-cuts, cutting corners and crossing public lawns.' And the expert should take this human weakness into consideration. Of course, a clear and methodical approach is a precondition. 'If one decides to compromise and leave the green spaces in the middle of high-density development to its own devices without any intervention, then a neglected, failed and horrible wilderness will

be the result.' 'When we are dealing with nature, let us not romanticize it excessively, as in that case we might as well return to dwelling in turf huts.' Mien Ruys, a truly sophisticated expert, recognized already the bad side effects of architectural gardening. 'Round 1930, after a period in which outward appearance set the tone, reflection on the essence of living, without any frills, began. Garden architecture followed a similar pattern. As an extension of the house, which is little more than a simple cubic structure with the inevitable windows and doors, a garden was created with straight fences round a perfectly manicured lawn, the whole planting consisting of a columnar conifer or a tall standing poplar. The house and its garden were identified as a whole and the contrast between the basic characteristics of either was forgotten.' This is what Mien Ruys stood for and so she set the pace that would later become a dominating factor shaping horticulture. As yet, Mien Ruys put the various trends in juxtaposition.

In public areas she preferred to see paving stones rather than parks that are poorly kept or not functioning properly, private gardens rather than a neglected park. Her recommendations for the layout of a garden can roughly be divided into three categories. First of all, advice to creative gardeners, people who use plants to achieve a particular image. Many evergreen, non-changing shrubs and hedges that can be trimmed in a specific shape. Her second recommendation was to gardeners who prefer a layout with profusely flowering perennials and shrubs, fragrance and colour all year round in a labour-intensive garden. Finally, advice for those garden owners who feel their garden is a reflection of nature, a peaceful biotope of man, plant and animal. If heather or dune is situated next to the house, why should you want to change that? It would be futile, says Mien Ruys, you would get either poor nature or a feeble garden.

The green world outside according to Bijhouwer

In that same book, Leven met groen [Living with Plants], Bijhouwer takes stock of the love of nature in the Netherlands and sets it off against a European perspective. In his opinion, the Dutch have utilized all the green available. Whereas there still are unspoilt high moors in Belgium, in the Netherlands these have been cut and forcibly turned into arable land with the help of an indecent amount of fertilizer. The Ruhr area is very densely populated, but at the same time there are vast areas of complete peace and quiet. However, in the Netherlands it is hard to find any scenic areas of a significant size near the towns. The automobile was not yet common property and a moped riders preferred to stay closer to the home. This, he explained, was the reason for the phenomenon of the sixties, roadside picnicking. The day tripper, getting away from the town, was not accustomed to peace and quiet and solitude. For that reason he did not want to be far away from transport, company and refreshments. In addition, plans for the reclamation of the Zuiderzeepolders were in full swing in the sixties. The manageability of agricultural industry on the new land was a top priority. Old, languid landscapes were made more efficient through land consolidation. According to Bijhouwer, our taste in respect of green spaces is not really surprising, since we take our aesthetic sense from a landscape we acquired artificially, we wrested it from the sea ourselves. A clear horizon with trees in orderly lines proves our superiority over the sea or over nature. The fact that in this expansion old landscapes perish or that the flood barrier in the Hollandse IJssel ruins the perspective of the old surrounding polder, is a consequence of unavoidable progress, even if it makes us sad.

Moerheim Gardening Catalogues 1960 and 1961

The Moerheim collection of 1960 could no longer be summed up in a single booklet. There were a number of small, colourful booklets listing top-class selections and commercial editions in many languages. The folder for the general public for 1960-1961 was a full-colour magazine. The outside cover showed an example of a garden with only ten species of plants. On page two an explanation was given. Much can be done with few resources. The recurring motto was: 'One alphabet is sufficient to write all books.' The explanation could be quite concise; after all, we had the magazine Onze Eigen Tuin [Our Own Garden], a magazine established in 1954 to serve all lovers of plants and flowers. It related 'everything from before planting to after planting to those who know and those who want to find out.' The catalogue still sang the praises of conifers: in the garden they are the finishing touch. Rock plants first, and then perennials. The complete catalogue serves as an order form. Buyers only needed to cross off what they wanted and return the catalogue. The rose catalogue: 'These are our roses and this is how we apply them', is quite lyrical in its descriptions of 'Soraya' or 'Grace of Monaco'. The 'Belle Blonde' is called 'as warm as ripe corn, so soaked with the sun is this rose'.

112

Moerheim Catalogue (1960)

Forestry Commission plan for range of dunes North Holland – opening salt pans (1963)

N.A. de Boer in collaboration with **A.J.M. de Jong, Public Works Department Emmen** town planning and
planting scheme Angerslo, Emmen (1960)

N.A. de Boer in collaboration with **A.J.M. de Jong, Public Works Department Emmen** town planning and
planting scheme Angerslo, Emmen (1960)

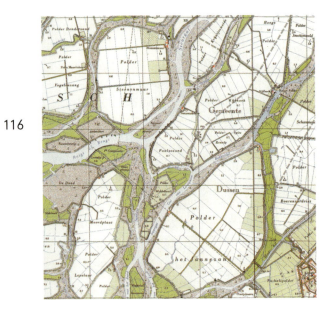

F.M. Maas landscaping plan for Altena-West, land consolidation (1967)

Groningen peat district De Wilderrank

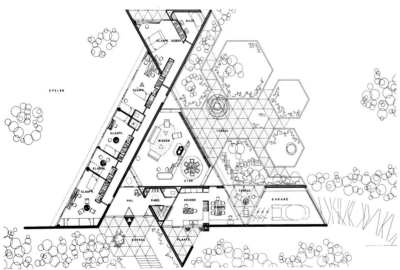

P.A.M. Buys bungalow garden, Eersel

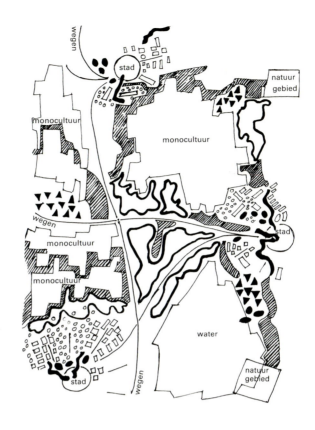

119

L. le Roy public garden Kennedylaan, Heerenveen (1966)

Tj.H. Koning   De Kempenhof, Domburg (1963)

Walenburg, Langbroek (1970)

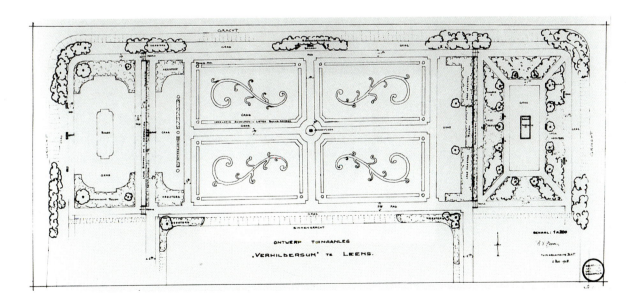

R.T. Boon Borg Verhildersum, Leens (1968)

1970-1980

122

• Green Star recreation areas • water ballet in Het Twiske • the unity of man and nature • land art enhances the landscape • gardens not in touch with Mother Earth • warming-up spots in Holy-Noord • plant liberation • gardening pioneers in Zeeland • roses triumphant and conifers fill compartments

Green Star before and after the oil crisis

As early as in 1936 Baanakkers and Het Twiske, two nature areas to the north of Amsterdam, had been bought on the advice of the Botanical Society. Het Twiske, a bird sanctuary, was drained in 1941 and as a result was lost as a waterfowl habitat. In 1967 the area was designated a 'Green Star' recreational area near the town following the master plan Structuurschets voor de ruimtelijke ontwikkeling van de openluchtrecreatie in Nederland [Master Plan for Planning Outdoor Recreation in the Netherlands], 1964. The map of the Second Policy Document on Physical Planning shows many Green Star Areas. These areas usually were former farming and stock breeding areas, redeveloped for mass day tripper recreation. All are easily accessible by car. Each Green Star Area was divided into zones, from quiet to popular to very popular zones. The first plan for Het Twiske radically ignored the original landscape, but in the end part of the original system of ditches was retained. Another part of the area was landscaped in traditional style as parkland with lawns bordered by trees. The oil crisis of 1972 marked a temporary setback (no cars, no visitors), but forecasts had to be adjusted anyway because the population growth was slower than had been expected.

Water ballet in Het Twiske

In 1971 landscape architect Mariska Pemmelaar designed a water playground for the Blauwe Poort, an area in Het Twiske that has been developed specifically for children. All aspects of water and games were joined in a 'playful' water ballet; it is a very popular spot. There is much variation within Het Twiske. In the wet outer parts birds nest in the reedy borders of the many islets, rarely disturbed by visitors. In other places, mostly within easy cycling distance from the towns of Oostzaan and Landsmeer, beaches were made that are popular with mothers who take their toddlers there to paddle in splash pools. Elsewhere jumble sales are held on Sundays while on the spacious lawn of 'Little Ankara' people picnic and barbecue right beside the many cars parked criss-cross along the edges.

The unity of man and nature

In his book Kunstig Landschap [Artful Landscape] the theologian C.W. Mönnich philosophizes about the bond between man and nature. To demonstrate this bond he considers the role of artists and writes: 'The landscape is always present in the minds of the people who have to live in it, whether they be primitive hunters, farmers, city folk, industrialists, proletarians, or whatever; it is their feeding territory. If we distinguish between town and country as if we were contrasting art and nature, we deceive ourselves. The unity between our environment and ourselves goes deeper and has more to do with our authenticity, our personality, than with any distinction between town and country or art and nature. Deep down the sense of unity with the world in which we live is present within us. It is the unity of nature, of which we happen to be part. Nature is always more novel than the latest novelty and will continue longer than any generation, invention or discovery. The new landscape is a part of us. It is the artist who have made this visible and who have communicated the bond, under the threat, the curse and the reconciliation, between an environment even if it is marked by industrialization, and its inhabitants.'

This long, woolly quote typifies the seventies: a search for the essence of nature and how man and his man-made factories and technology fit in. Wealth and prosperity versus well-being.

Land art below sea level

Studying the history of art we may observe how idealized glorification of nature developed from Renaissance times far into the Romantic era. In the nineteenth century social realism already introduced potato eaters and industry. Abstractionism and conceptual art followed, and in the 1960s nature itself became the subject of a movement going by the name of land art. The point of departure for this time-bound phenomenon was to raise awareness of 'the place in the landscape'. The landscapes of the new Flevopolder, land without a visual history and in need of an identity and recognizability, were ideal for experimenting with shapes and forms. Some remarkable examples of land art can still be viewed, such as the Observatory by Robert Morris, which he built in 1971 for the 'Sonsbeek Buiten de Perken' sculpture exhibition in Arnhem. Land art artists do not place their sculptures at random but visually incorporate the surroundings. For Robert Morris, Flevoland's main feature was its wide open spaces. The visual axes of the Observatory are derived from light incidence, the time of day and the position of the sun, all according to ancient Inca ideas. As at the modern ritual held at Stonehenge, at the special Sunsation festival, revellers greet the sun when it rises after the shortest night of the year. At midwinter solstice on 21 December the sun can be seen rising through a V-shaped opening. Strangely, the Observatory is situated near two busy roads, which disturb the contemplative character of the experience both audibly and visually. Aerial photographs show the beautiful layout, but at eye level the aesthetic effect is not quite as impressive.

Also in Flevoland lies Aardzee [Earth Sea] created by Piet Slegers. It is the largest work of art in the Netherlands and took the artist seven years to complete (1975-1982). This 'experiential landscape' is hidden behind an earthen wall and is accessible to visitors in two places across cattle grid bridges. The diagonal lines are consciously incongruous with the strictly right-angled lines of the fields. Sleger's inspiration for this interplay of lines came from land reclamation, the 'victory of man over water'. Aardzee is a play with sloping planes and changing incidences of light meant to evoke awareness of sky and earth, light and darkness, in a flat, wide open expanse stretching to the distant, empty horizon.

Robert Smithson's Broken Circle, near Emmen in the province of Drenthe, consists of an Ice Age megalith grave placed in a sandpit on a spit of land. A semicircular ditch was dug beside it and a spiralling lookout was built. The landscape itself supplied the material.

Gardens not in touch with Mother Earth

Le Corbusier once had a brilliant idea. If we were to build all new buildings on stilts we would not steal land from ecological systems. Vegetation could continue uninterrupted between the concrete columns, rainwater could run off naturally into the soil and people would be more in touch with nature. In the year 1970 cities presented a rather different view, dominated by buildings with few quiet spaces in between and with plenty of noise and stench to boot. A counter-movement set in. Parts of cities were closed off for motorized vehicles and huge stone tubs for small trees and seasonal plants appeared on pavements.

Town-dwellers as well as visitors wished for green areas round the corner. Post-World War II neighbourhoods with high-rise blocks as well as traditional pre-war quarters were assessed for their recreational potential. Lampposts were fitted out with hanging baskets, tubular constructions on heavy metal feet supported whole families of plants. Boats, façades, pavements… everything was a potential garden candidate, not least the roofs of office buildings, factories and multi-storey car parks. Balconies were enlarged and 'turned to the sun' to make them suitable for carrying robust vegetation. This kind of container gardening cut off from the open ground required a specialized approach. Soil type, artificial drainage, artificial fertilization, and artificial watering all together formed a complex package of requirements demanding much knowledge and maintenance, and so money. Funds were available, the economy being strong. The head offices of both the AMRO and the ABN banks were furnished with impressive roof gardens. The ABN building was also equipped with broad balconies from which hanging gardens overhung the street below. In Amsterdam-West a 1200 m^2 roof no-visitors garden was laid out on top of a multi-storey car park to provide a pleasant view to the people living in the high-rise buildings around it.

Holy-Noord nature park

Holy-Noord, in Vlaardingen, is neither open country nor a traditional city park. It is a kind of 'eco-block' enclosed in a suburb on a raised terrain including a rubble hill on which the city's Parks and Gardens Department has tried to create an interesting landscape. The park is divided into sections – a herb garden, butterfly meadow, dune strip, Zeeland dike, orchid island, flora from Limburg, manor plants; a whole range of vulnerable mini-ecosystems. The sections have been planted with varying degrees of success. Human intervention in this complex eco-park depends on the knowledge of the gardeners and ecologists responsible, who have plenty of problems to face. What is good for the plants may be disastrous in terms of water management; breeding lapwings and dogs do not go well together; the spring meadow with its bright red poppies has to be mown at the right time or even worked with rotary cultivators. For the butterflies low 'warming-up spots' have been made. Holy-Noord's specialized gardeners are aware that Holy-Noord's fate is wholly in their hands.

Plant liberation

The all-too-streamlined manner of gardening described above called for a reaction, which came from growers and horticulturists stressing the pluriformity of plant life. Plants needed to be 'liberated', in sixties jargon. Human control of green areas and gardens through mechanization and streamlining was to be turned into a symbiotic relationship, a dialogue with nature. Mutual respect and room for growth was essential to this. In fact this was nothing new; such ideas were quite common up to about 1900, when garden owners and head gardeners decided how gardens were to be planted on the basis of handed-down knowledge. The extensive catalogues of the seventies listed almost forgotten species as well as new varieties. The possibility of buying plants in pots becomes popular and visits to nurseries were no longer restricted to the flowering month, which led to a strengthening of personal ties between customers and growers. Some growers brought unusual plants or their seeds on the market, serving a new generation of home gardeners who thought in terms of plants rather than concepts. What with greater environmental awareness and more people owning small gardens, gardening was approached in a new, mostly small-scale way. The catalogues of these 'traditional' growers became highly specialized plant lists with lengthy, lyrical descriptions of the plants.

Zeeland's garden pioneers

If plants were in need of liberation, then certainly garden architecture must be. In reaction to the ideas of 'feasibility' in the sixties and structures imposed by authorities a new style of gardening arose. No ready-made solutions anymore, no longer the extension of an architectural vision with beds to be filled in at whim, but mini-biotopes that were the continuous creation of the gardener as he learned from experience and in which plants and animals could feel 'at home'. Influences from abroad, especially England, were strong. Vita Sackville-West's garden Sissinghurst became a veritable place of pilgrimage. From Sissinghurst people took home ideas and plants to Walcheren in Zeeland, where a group of ladies laid out a number of gardens, which became models for many other gardens. The pioneering ladies experimented with garden design, soil improvement and ecology. Which plants grow best on which type of soil, how does one keep the heavy clay soil of Zeeland permeable, which trees and shrubs are most suitable for windbreaks, which birds and butterflies are attracted by these trees and shrubs? The type of garden that was to become the most popular in the Netherlands originated in Zeeland. Madeleine van Bennekom's clay soil garden De Kempen-hof in Domburg may serve as an example. She is gardening on clay soil from 1967. After looking around for a while, van Bennekom came into contact with Mien Ruys and Hetty Cox, two expert plant breeders at the time. Tjaard Koning made a draft plan and a farmer called Provoost sowed the grass. Plants were tested for 'acid' or 'lime' and the soil was enriched and fertilized accordingly. Next, the garden borders were filled with colourful flowering plants; many grey-white and blue-white ones and fewer red-orange plants. Some plants took root, but others withered, in spite of intensive daily care. Some monardas established themselves but the camelias from England did not survive. In this way a gardening world came into existence where grass lane, shrub garden, island bed developed their own individuality and still blended harmoniously. The other three pioneer gardens of Zeeland are De Tintelhof, Slot der Nisse and the garden of the Lenshoek family in Kloetinge.

Plant Breeders' Catalogue 1970

The Moerheim plant catalogue for 1970 lists no fewer than 750 plant species. The nursery employs a staff of thirty people, ready to come and plant them in your garden. The large, full-colour catalogue lists 'stars of old who continue their march of victory', such as iris, astilbe, viburnum, weigelia, spiraea, epidemium and many varieties of conifers. A second catalogue

lists 'protected' varieties of roses. Breeding its own varieties, Moerheim attached great importance to high quality and 'authenticity'. The whole catalogue breathed a modern, streamlined approach, standardization and strong species in their selection of plants. Target groups at this time consisted of businesses, municipalities and institutions. The abovementioned conifers met all requirements: evergreen, full, retaining their shape, requiring little maintenance. They are popular plants for filling beds.

Moerheim Catalogue (1970)

M. Pemmelaar-Groot   recreation area Het Twiske, water playground for the Blauwe Poort, Oostzaan (1972)

M. Pemmelaar-Groot, T. van Keulen (Grontmij NV)   recreation area Het Twiske, between Oostzaan, Landsmeer and Den Ilp (1967)

P. van Loon recreation area Gaasperplas (1971)

WIJKPARK 'HOLY-NOORD'
GEM. VLAARDINGEN

Public Works Department Vlaardingen nature park Holy-Noord, Vlaardingen (1977)

R. Morris 'Observatory', Lelystad (1971)

P. Slegers 'Aardzee', Zeewolde (1977)

Roof garden on garage, Rijswijkstraat, Amsterdam (situation 2002)

1980-1990

Dividing and sharing green areas

The eighties were a very prosperous period. Many people could afford to buy or sell a house or to refurnish their home or garden, and many did. All Dutch landscapes had by now been mapped, policy documents were drafted and ideas were collected in reports. The question was whether to preserve everything as it was or to try new, more dynamic avenues. To think 'green' was popular and politically correct. Businesses rediscovered the garden as a marketing instrument; societies were founded for the protection or enjoyment of parks and gardens.

Garden societies

In 1980 a small group of garden lovers founded the Nederlandse Tuinenstichting [Dutch Garden Foundation]. They were concerned about the fact that, due to expansion of towns and villages, gardens were lost which were characteristic for a certain region, period or garden architect on account of their location, layout or plants. Several gardening societies already existed, as well as two magazines, Groei en Bloei [Growth and Bloom] and Onze Eigen Tuin [Our Own Garden] which provided tips and advice (e.g. how to deal with aphids or red spider mite) to a faithful readership of plant lovers. The Garden Foundation was the first society to concentrate solely on the form and content of garden design. Under the energetic leadership of Arend Jan van der Horst the society inventoried threatened gardens, provided subsidies, gave support in the shape of publicity, and awarded grants to art historians for research into Dutch garden architecture after 1850.

Sissinghurst still the favourite

In the eighties Dutch garden design was strongly influenced by the English art of gardening. In a poll, two out of three garden owners mentioned Sissinghurst as the main source of their ideas. Dividing the garden into compartments – green sections enclosed by hedges of yew, box or beech – offers lots of possibilities and is very suitable to the Dutch landscape. In urban environments hedges can be used to shut out views of the less attractive surroundings and to provide a rural feeling. In the countryside, on the other hand, hedges offer protection against the cold north wind and shelter, while openings can be made for vistas of a cow meadow or a distant church spire.

A broader range of plants

Exotic plants became more popular for plant beds and borders. Information about plants and gardens was easily accessible thanks to the many gardening books published, both Dutch books and translations of English books. Garden trips to England remained popular and when cable television was introduced in the Netherlands the BBC programme Gardeners' World attracted Dutch viewers too. As the demand for unusual plants increased, colour schemes for borders became increasingly refined. Flourishing gardening magazines described the range of colouring in Ton ter Linden's garden in Ruinen in lyrical tones. Combinations of wild plants and cultivars and combinations of bulbous plants, annuals and perennials made for greater differentiation.

132

Garden centres expand their activities

There was a growing interest in green spaces, environment and gardening. A diversity of developments, such as featureless large-scale neighbourhoods, dwindling wilderness areas and travels to other countries and their gardening cultures, inspired many people to create small back gardens for recreation. Garden centres broadened their range of plants and services. Apart from offering a wider range of unusual plants, they also began to sell garden furniture, garden torches and nesting boxes.

Special gardens for specific groups

Educational and recreational aspects of the art of gardening became more prominent during the eighties. Mien Ruys' model gardens in Dedemsvaart, by now traditional, and Rob Herwig's gardens in Lunteren were as popular as ever. Garden centres too embraced specialization and diversification, offering something for everyone – large gardens, small gardens, scent gardens for the blind, flower boxes at hip height for wheelchair gardeners. Ada Hofman's series of Water Gardens demonstrated all kinds of possibilities in this area, from mini bog gardens and rain barrels to large ponds.

The garden became an extension of the living room, with sunken sitting areas equipped with a barbecue set and a stone grill. Cocooning 'came out' and sometimes led to frumpiness. In the words of garden reviewer Romke van de Kaa, each home had its own miniature Versailles.

Interdisciplinary gardens

Sharing garden pleasure was another novelty of this period. Open Days, Gardening Weekends and Garden Fairs were introduced and sculpture garden sightseeing routes set out. Public garden tours were organized with an opera performance or a concert included. Good fun and an opportunity for socializing.

Professionals, too, 'peeped over the fence'. Architects, garden architects, landscape architects, artists, local and regional authorities and property developers co-operated more often than they had done before. Architects designed gardens, artists built summer houses and grottoes; democracy and participation extending to gardening and landscaping. Limited space required careful consultation.

Regional activities

Garden Days were organized and garden routes set out in many regions. The northern provinces of Groningen, Friesland and Drenthe issued guides listing gardens open to visitors. In Limburg, in the south, a handful of gardeners gave a new impulse to garden culture and several private gardens were opened to the general public. One of these was Ineke Greve's garden at Huys De Dohm. The garden is famous for the meticulous care lavished on it. A strict alternating pattern is applied in the various compartments. Perfectly manicured gardens with classical vases, enclosed by box hedges, alternate with colourful kitchen gardens displaying bright reds and deep purples. The lemon thyme bed has been trimmed to perfection. This is 'ultimate gardening', controlling nature to the square inch or, in Greve's own words, gardening as top-class sport. Other gardeners, less demanding, made beautiful gardens too. Jan van Opstal and Jo Willems in their garden Heerenhof, in Maastricht, experimented with traditional dahlias, tuberous begonias and rye to create strong colour contrasts with highly refined cultivars. Patricia van Roosmalen in her garden in Rekem, designed by Mr and Mrs Canneman, playfully set off colourful golden elms against a dark green weather house made of cornel. Although the great majority of gardens, then as now, were the work of enthusiastic amateurs who put much loving effort into them, garden architects became more prominent and more involved as designers of home gardens during the eighties. They had competition from experienced garden owners who had designed their own gardens and offered their services. The profession of garden architect is not protected by law.

Freer garden design

The freer, more natural approach to garden design gained ground, quite literally. This free approach held that gardens should have 'wild plantings within a strong design'. Seeds may grow where they fall, plants may grow where they stand. Two gardeners in the province of Overijssel, Piet Oudolf and Henk Gerritsen, took these principles very seriously in their garden Priona, a wild garden on a Saxon farm, with matching fauna. They wrote a book explaining their philosophy. Oudolf, a grower better known as a garden architect, with his wife Anja introduced new plant varieties and put these on show in his private garden in Hummelo. Oudolf favoured the year-round cycle. He did not choose plants solely on the basis of their time of flowering and flower shapes. He experimented with 'neighbouring' plants, interacting clusters. Here, leaf shape, autumn coloration and winter structure under snow play an important role. Since his experiments monardas and grasses have found their way into many a garden. Oudolf's plant days for select groups of people were the precursors of the fairs that were organized later. Mainly English guests such as Penelope Hobhouse and Christopher Lloyd would tell the audience about their gardening experiences.

New designs in an old tradition

The eighties also saw a reaction to the free designs and fixation on plants of the designers of the seventies. Young landscape architects were tired of regulation and control and wanted to make sweeping gestures. Their great desire was to make designs in a grand old tradition, with park entrance avenues a mile long and lined by double rows of trees. Or, as at the Prinsenlandpark in Rotterdam, designed by Bureau Bakker en Bleeker, a rectangular park lined with a full four kilometres of cherry trees. In short, the soft, rounded designs of the previous period with its attention to detail were succeeded by a clear, 'angular' style which harked back to the New Garden Designs practised by Warnau, Boer and Bijhouwer in the fifties and sixties. The

Prinsenlandpark has wide green lawns, transparent structures and open views. The sports fields, the hippodrome, the swimming pool and the children's farm are easily identifiable. When the wind blows in the park, you were meant to feel it. At the same time, there is plenty of scope for variation within the quadrangles.

The restoration of palace Het Loo

During the seventies an interesting debate was carried on concerning restoration of the garden of palace Het Loo. This English landscape style garden had remained unchanged since the death of Princess Wilhelmina, the former Queen. Meandering paths led through a park-like terrain with vistas towards exceptional stands of trees, and there was a small cabin for painting. The debate did not turn on restoration itself but on the question to which period. In view of the festivities planned for 1984 in commemoration of William and Mary, a seventeenth century formal garden was proposed. But why turn a perfectly beautiful park upside down? Why cut down venerable old beeches to make place for flowerbeds in classical style? Apart from this, which plants were used in the late seventeenth century, where to find them, and what about the costs of laying out a very labour-intensive garden when labour was increasingly expensive? Nevertheless, in 1975 a classical garden was decided on. The restoration was finished in time and baron van Asbeck and his work force made an excellent job of it. Het Loo is once again a fine example of a seventeenth century palace garden, as well as an example of a Dutch garden in French style. The present gardens are at least as famous as their predecessors and attract many visitors.

'Makable' landscapes

A similar debate took place on a broader scale. Expansion of agriculture had already increased the uniformity of the countryside. Apart from the need for larger parcels, referred to earlier, there was the desire to preserve characteristic features in landscapes. Such features might include a sand drift near Kootwijk, a polder like the Beemster or an unused railroad crossing in Groesbeek. In view of the ever increasing pressure on the countryside virtually everything was regarded as a scenery, even 'non-lieux' [non-places] such as motorways and industrial estates. The discussion was simple. One group sees the Netherlands as a 'makable' country. If we want more green areas we can make them, and if we need more storage space for surplus water we can flood river foreland. The other side is not so sure about makability. To restore the island Tiengemeten to nature, for example, farmers and other inhabitants would have to be removed from the island. Or, if you want a dune valley to flow over naturally into tidal movement, is that really worth two million Euro?

A framework plan

In 1987 a book titled Het Plan Ooievaar [The Stork Plan] was published which dealt with the future of the great rivers area. In keeping with the spirit of the times a 'framework plan' was presented. 'Present values are less important than the natural potential of the river area. Old natural components must be restored to their original relationship and the dynamics of the river will be the driving force.' In other words, separation where necessary and connections ('interweaving') where possible. For the first time they did not regard what was but what might be. Land outside the dikes was intended as nature area, land inside the dikes was for agricultural use. The idea was that these two types of land use should co-exist and not be opposed to each other. A direct result of the plan was the realization of the project De Blauwe Kamer [The Blue Room] on land adjacent to the river Rhine, near Rhenen. The summer dike was cut to create pools inside the dike. It was hoped that a variant of the old floodplain forest would grow up on the former grasslands and orchards. Horses and cattle were imported to keep the grass on the spring meadows short. The area is open to visitors for walking and there is an information centre.

Landmarks

Landscape architects from Wageningen University regard Holland's present landscapes, resulting from land reclamations and divisions, as 'unique and very beautiful'. They reject the nostalgic motivations underpinning many regional landscape plans. A landscape should reflect the lifestyle of its inhabitants, so medieval parcels from Roman times should be dispensed with. For some artists, however, the new polders of Flevoland were too bare and too anonymous. They wanted to build landmarks to serve as beacons in the dull, monotonous landscape. Visual artist Marinus Boezem proposed a living design that would grow and develop in harmony with its surroundings; new land needs to acquire a history. The Green Cathedral he designed has poplars representing columns and the sky forms the roof. After all, the first primitive temples were just forest clearings. Boezem's cathedral presents a different sight every season, while it will also change over the years. The process is important, not the moment in time. The Forestry Commission's designs for traffic intersections were more prosaic. The planting plan for the large cloverleaf intersection at Vianen is such that the motorist drives through varied vegetation with open and closed groups of trees. This gives the motorist a sense of protection, as if driving through an age-old environment. This feeling, experienced today, was already provi-ded for us in 1980.

Corporate gardens

Gardens may also serve commercial purposes. In the eighties companies laid out gardens with an eye to public relations. The nature of the company determined the choice of architect. In 's Hertogenbosch, Mien Ruys' bureau designed a geometrical garden for the Postal Services (PTT). At the distributing centre a narrow strip has been reserved for plantings. A geometrical pattern of square privet hedges encloses the terrain to create an austere green counterweight to the large building. The width of the hedge-squares was determined by how far a gardener holding shears can reach. The paths, paved with common paving stones, are also characteristic of this design of the Nieuwe Bouwen.

Jorn Copijn provided the new organically designed office building of KPMG with a 'nature-inspired' office garden and a community park, and did the same for the new NMB Bank office. In both buildings, which were designed by the architect Ton Albers, bamboo bushes and spontaneous vegetation set the scene. Lode-wijk Baljon, a specialist in park design and a proponent of 'lush open spaces for reflection on one's own thoughts', made a more austere design with fruit trees, roses, irises and laven-der for the office garden of Ahold in Zaandam. By now many large concerns consider a well-designed garden an effective marketing tool.

Museumpark

In 1988 the Office for Metropolitan Architec-ture and Yves Brunier were jointly commis-sioned to landscape an area in Rotterdam situ-ated between four museums – Boijmans Van Beuningen Museum, the Netherlands Archi-tecture Institute, the Natural History Museum and the Kunsthal – 'as if they were best rooms', to create a spatial highlight, similar to the Schouwburgplein and the Boompjes. The various parts of the Museum-park look like entrances to a public area, a courtyard for the museums of Rotterdam. Artificiality is the leit-motiv. Huge mirrors, gravelled spaces with small white-painted fruit trees for cultural events, an open-air theatre and a bridge across a stagnant Japa-nese brook are essential ele-ments in the general plan. Walking from one museum to the next one's senses are stimulated in other ways too. From the bridge carpets of colourful flowers should be visible throughout the year. This is a city park reflecting urban life. It is not a buffer zone between the four museums, nor is it an extension of any of these. Rather, it is a self-willed, intentionally random, autonomous space.

The Cruydthoeck Seed List

'If the flowering comes to nought, the proper way you were not taught.' This is one of the sayings enlivening the Cruydthoeck's seed list of wild plants for 1979-1980. This well-written catalogue, with hand-made paper cover, con-tains information about indigenous plants, a 'wild plants' bibliography and articles about medicinal herbs, dye plants, apiculture and semi-wild gardens, and poetry by Ida Gerhardt ('Het landschap staat in mij geschreven' [Land-scape written in me]), Elly de Waard and Jan Hendrik Leopold and some fine woodcuts. The alphabetical index lists 486 plants, from Achil-lea millefolium (yarrow) to Veronica spicata (spiked speedwell). The Cruydthoeck was set up by Rob Leopold and Dick van der Burg, who were inspired by ideals from the sixties. Rob and his wife Ans owned a boutique, Mandela, in the city of Groningen, where they sold, among other things, Dick's hand-made sandals. They were given the opportunity to take over a nursery and so they landed on the farm in 1978. Their love of nature in all its manifestations and inter-relationships has been the driving force behind their pioneering activities. The seed list is up-dated every year, not only with new plants but also with anything related to gardening. And of course, poetry and sayings like, 'If we care about nature we do not sow in nature!'

Cruydthoeck (1980)

136

P. and **A. Oudolf** turn their garden and nursery in Hummelo into a breeding ground of new varieties of plants

The castle gardens in Arcen are a book of quotations of gardening styles and atmospheres

I. Greve the ultimate refinement in the art of gardening, Huys De Dohm, Heerlen (1980)

J. van Opstal and **J. Willems** turned the Heerenhof in Maastricht into a colour laboratory; black tulips, red dahlias and a field of barley

P. van Roosmalen Rekem

H. Njio distances himself from all gardening trends with his very personal ideas on gardening in Bemelen

143

H. Gerritsen and **A. Schlepers** create their Priona gardens with 'wild dream' plants (1983)

A. Hofman specialized water flora garden, Loozen (1987)

The large-scale restoration of the palace gardens of Het Loo by **J.B. baron Van Asbeck** triggered a discussion on the saving and conservation of monumental nature (1984))

With its 'shell' views the Plan Ooievaar provides new possibilities for the present landscape. A plan developed by

D. de Bruin, D. Hamhuis, L. van Nieuwenhuijze, O.W. Overmars, D. Sijmons and **F. Vera** (1986)

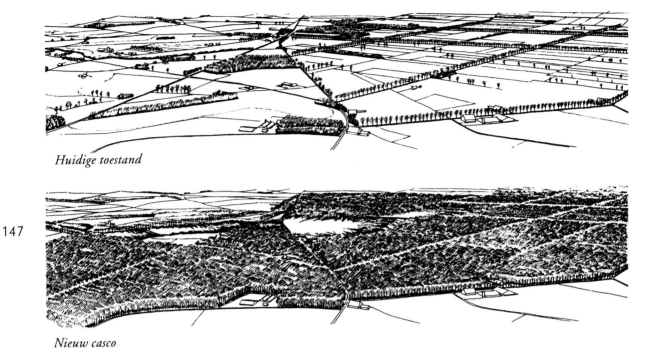

Huidige toestand

147

Nieuw casco

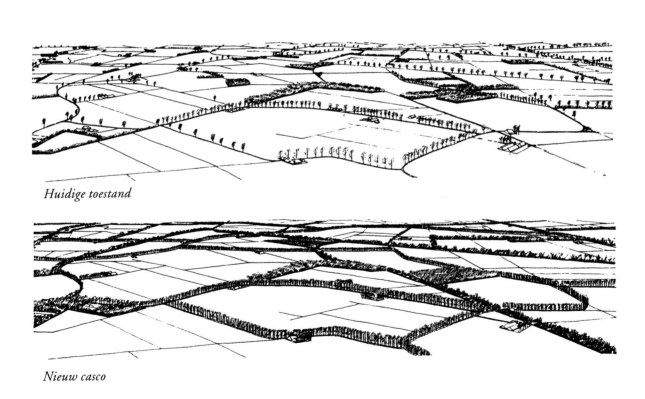

Huidige toestand

Nieuw casco

With its 'shell' views the Plan Ooievaar provides new possibilities for the present landscape. A plan developed by
D. de Bruin, D. Hamhuis, L. van Nieuwenhuijze, O.W. Overmars, D. Sijmons and **F. Vera** (1986)

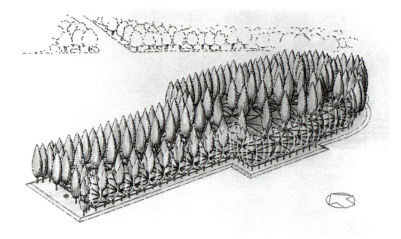

M. Boezem built a transitory, history-making 'Green Cathedral', Almere-Haven (1987)

149

Town Planning Department Rotterdam in collaboration with **Bureau B+B town planning and landscape architecture**   Prinsenland, Rotterdam (1991-1998)

OMA/R. Koolhaas, Y. Brunier   Museumpark, Rotterdam (1988-1989)

Bureau Ruys Veldhoen   design for a field near the forwarding centre of the PTT, 's-Hertogenbosch (1987)

L. Baljon   garden at Ahold head office, Zaandam (1988)

Copijn Utrecht Gardening Consultants indoor gardens and roof gardens ING Bank, Amsterdam-Zuidoost

(1980-1986)

• Everything is garden, everything is landscape
• hydrography comes first • enclosed gardens are
back • a city park with few plants • a new approach
to old forms • away with prickly ornamental shrubs
• highway follies • museum square and museum
garden • design specialisms • a modern country
estate • a unified vision on many designs • a recreational park and a work of art • the Forestry
Commission • everything is a garden, or is it?
•Plant Shop Bulletin

Hydrography comes first

Population pressure, urban sprawl, increase
of noise nuisance and light nuisance at night,
all of this led to the awareness that open space,
absolute quiet and pitch-darkness were matters
to be taken very seriously. Town and country
planners had already spent much thought on
the functions of green areas and expansion
zones, and spatial planning documents covered
many yards of shelf space. Pressure on the
landscape forced planners to be creative, taking
into regard the many interests. Whatever the
plan or project, co-operation was essential.
In the Netherlands water management is all-
important. The present system is the result of
many centuries of evolution and is recorded in
a hydrographic chart. The land is subsiding and
the sea level is rising, so more water has to be
drained off. Rainwater is retained for a shorter
period and flows away less easily. Fixed infrastructure like the road system and railways
play a role in determining the size of housing
estates and meadows, and about these basic
principles there is a lot to decide. For example,
no new housing can be planned in river flood-
plains if these are to be used for storage of
surplus water.

Any local plan made by a garden or landscape architect is embedded in regional and
national plans. Planners and architects thought
along with government agencies and offered
pioneering ideas and solutions. MVRDV for
example, a firm of architects and landscape
designers, has designed architectural 'stacks' of
all kinds, including nature. The much acclaimed
Dutch Pavilion at the World Exhibition 2000 in
Hanover consisted of four stacked landscapes
topped by a windmill. Another futuristic design
shows storeys of woods and bulb-fields stacked
on top of each other, with pigsties on the four-
teenth floor. The sties have private balconies
where our prospective chops can take a breath
of fresh air.

Enclosed gardens are back

Garden layout and design also adapted to the
increasing hustle and bustle of city life. Views
from gardens became clogged with high-rises,
industrial buildings and lighting masts. People
started looking inward, gardens became more
restrained; small, sober spaces to relax in a busy
urban melting pot became important. Spiritual
trends such as Zen and Feng Shui inspired emp-
tier, transparent gardens. The garden designed
by Michael van Gessel on the Herengracht in
Amsterdam is an example of the new trend. In
long and narrow gardens diagonal or meandering paths are usually made and the garden is
raised or sunk, or divided into compartments.
To be able to see the garden as a whole was a
taboo in the eighties. But not to van Gessel. He
made a pond over the full length of the garden
and the back end of the garden is clearly visible
from the house. Left and right of the pond paths
starting near the house below water level, run
up to a bench at the back of the garden.

Green initiatives

Interest in smaller gardens translated itself
into all kinds of initiatives. The Stichting de
Amsterdamse Grachtentuin [Amsterdam Garden

Foundation], founded in 1992, inventoried canal house gardens, drew attention to green areas along the city canals, converted built-in garages into green oases and published a series of books, one per canal, in which the gardens are described and reviewed.

In Rotterdam, Architecture International Rotterdam (AIR) organized a series of projects in which an architect and an artist from various cultures were requested to co-operate and give their views on the future of urban greenscaping. This resulted in an exhibition, opening of parks to the public, a book and a series of engaging lectures and polemics.

A traditional garden in modern guise
In 1994 Els Proost designed a formal representative garden for the Vormgevingsinstituut [Netherlands Design Institute] on the Keizersgracht in Amsterdam. In conformity with the austere lines of the exhibition halls the outdoor area has been arranged in a similarly austere and orderly fashion. The garden presents a pleasing view from inside the building and on varnishing days is pleasant to sit or walk in and discuss the work shown. The garden is laid out in good Mien Ruys tradition, right-angled and sober with strong plants, a traditional lawn, common paving stones and Dutch clinkers, 'leaf shape is leaf function' – but the benches, tables and pergolas breathe Japan. Practical eclecticism in an oasis on the canal.

A city park with few plants
In a new housing estate in the Kop van Zuid area in Rotterdam, two 'spaces' designed by atelier Quadrat reflect a contemporary approach to urban planning. In one location a square facing the river has been panoramically enhanced by a spacious layout with copper lacquered boulders and fifteen silver lindens. The leaves of the lindens glisten beautifully in windy weather. At the other location a square space between two high-rises is taken up by a two-level trapezium-shaped lawn, a light-sculpture and a ramp, all this without obstructing views of the harbour.

No wishy-washy romanticism here; if the wind blows you should feel it.

A neo-neoclassical garden on a country estate
Combining old and new may lead to interesting results. In close co-operation with the architect and the residents of the Buitenplaats in Eelde, Jorn Copijn, the descendant of an old family of gardeners, designed a garden between a new organic brick museum building and a sixteenth century country estate. On the side of the older building he made a 'neo-neoclassical' design. A serpentine wall with classical trained fruit trees and a rose arbour above a fragrant lavender border flank a large pond with a Greek folly. There is an unexpected twist when the box and yew hedges suddenly begin to wave and meander, as if the design had become intoxicated. Swaying on, the apotheosis at the museum consists of sloping grassland and a wild-meadow roof garden. The bank of the ditch serves as an amphitheatre for the concert terrace on the opposite side. Dry walls by the artist Pieter Jan Kuiken connect the modern museum to the old church behind it. The garden time machine is working overtime in Eelde.

No prickly or ornamental plants for Schiphol Airport
Landscape architects no longer limited themselves to the countryside and green spaces. Bureau West 8 attracted attention with its plans for dividing the whole country into progressive and conservative zones, each with their corresponding ministries. Airports and industrial areas (Rijnmond, Betuwelijn) versus dormitory suburbs (Heemstede, Wassenaar), development versus conservation, areas of activity versus 'passive' areas. The corporate garden of insurance company Interpolis in Tilburg falls into the 'active' category. The garden, which has open spaces, surrounds a floating high-rise. Planking, gravel paths, pine trees and ponds set the scene. The garden is part of the flexible working space system. Employees can reserve workplaces per

half day and if the weather is fine they can take their notebooks outside and log on in a pine tree. Formal clarity also marks the plans Bureau West 8 made for Schiphol Airport. No 'gardenesque' prickly ornamental shrubs but, as a counterweight to the massive advertising columns featuring Sony and Marlboro, large numbers of birch trees are planted in all remaining areas and they form a counterbalance of green quietness. Dark underpasses are brightened up in 'Zen' style. The tender green colours of the birch foliage and flowering serviceberries soften the hard structures. All this is conducive to a healthy airborne image. Birds hate birches and the clover undergrowth is self-fertilizing. A very Dutch design.

Highway follies

Highways and slip roads were fitted into the landscape. For many road users highways merely carry you from A to B and are obstacles to be got over as quickly as possible. Verges were landscaped and contrasts with the surroundings were softened. Many highways cut through old landscapes, dividing estates. How to provide added value? Anne Mieke Backer believed the process could be reversed. She placed remnants of country estates in the loops of slip roads, creating anachronistic illusions; a kitchen garden, an old greenhouse, a folly.

To enhance existing landscapes with works of art had become a tradition, especially in the new Flevolands. Here the architect Daniel Libeskind and the sculptor Richard Serra designed works of art on square plots, 5 hectare (12 acres) in size. Libeskind's imaginary lines connected parts of Europe and worked this out in canals; a stretched-out, many-faced sculpture, crossed by a footpath.

Museum square and museum garden

To combine old and new became a regular task for architects. They often took the contrast as their point of departure. To support the 'dialogue' between the new building and its predecessor the remaining outdoor areas were usually filled in new, sometimes surprising ways. In collaboration with Ben van Berkel, who likes sloping surfaces, the garden and landscape architect Lodewijk Baljon conceived an empty front garden for the Rijksmuseum Twente. Or almost empty. No eye-catchers but sloping surfaces and gravel beds; a quiet place in the midst of busy, amorphous surroundings.

The architect Sven Ingvar Andersson was faced with a hard task in Amsterdam, where he made a master plan for the redevelopment of the Museum Square. The city council nibbled off bits on all sides for extensions of the Stedelijk Museum of Modern Art and the Van Gogh Museum, an entrance to the underground car park, a souvenir shop and a restaurant. Having taken all requirements into regard Andersson designed a large multifunctional lawn. Behind the Rijksmuseum the pond, planned a century earlier, was finally sunk, but the playground with plane trees was left as it was. An axis was created across the square and one has a strong sense of space. On the sloping roof garden of the adjacent Albert Heijn supermarket Amsterdammers basking in the sun contentedly criticize the designer.

Design specialisms

Thanks to the broad interest in green spaces and the resulting stream of orders and commissions, landscape architects could specialize. Robert Broekema designed many canal gardens in Amsterdam and Niek Roozen's name often appeared in connection with national entries in competitions abroad. Roozen's completed projects include many gardens that were part of Dutch contributions to exhibitions abroad – Munich, Liverpool, Stoke-on-Trent, Osaka and Stuttgart to name a few. He designed castle gardens in Arcen, was involved in the Floriade exhibitions of 1982 and 1992 and made the master plan for the 2002 Floriade in Hoofddorp. Roozen is also one in a long line of distinguished landscape architects who shaped the Westbroekpark in The Hague. L.P. Zocher drafted plans for this park as early as 1883. In 1920 Pieter Westbroek designed, and later realized, a park in landscape style. Poortman made his recommendations in 1923. In 1948, S.G.A. Doorenbos made a rosarium in the park, where important exhibitions are held to this day. Niek Roozen designed the National Perennials Garden, a show garden for Dutch growers, in 1977. The present Westbroekpark looks like an accumulation of designs, interests, modifications and other circumstances.

A modern country estate

Old country estates were examined for their strengths. Bureau Bosch and Slabbers took a hard look at the Manteling, a string of connected estates in Walcheren (Zeeland). Old structures from various periods were assessed for specific values. Next it was decided what was to be preserved, restored or renewed and a management plan was drawn up. This approach reflected a growing awareness that there is no point in conservation for sentimental reasons. Development, progress, evolution if you like, should not be obstructed, however beautiful the woods of the Manteling might be, and however pleasant the cool canopied pathways on a warm summer's day. It may be necessary at times to disrupt an existing park to make way for new developments. Of course, not everybody was enamoured by this sparkling long-term vision. Today's landscape is a certainty while tomorrow's possibilities are just that. For the first time in the twentieth century it was proposed to lay out new country estates. Revaluation of the concept 'country house' led to a number of new plans, one of which suited the landscape structure of Westhove. Modern, open and transparent design replaced the architecture of the old castle and the orchard is now on lease.

A unified vision on several old designs

At Twickel, the largest private country estate in the Netherlands, situated in the province of Overijssel, less desirable developments took place. The estate was subject to encroachment from all sides, the most brazen intruder being the ring road around Delden. This road broke up the classical pattern of lanes, even crossing the drive, which formed the natural connection between the castle to the one side, and the village, gate buildings and coach houses to the other side. Apart from this, a car park was planned in an open field and many trees that were part of the original layout had reached their peak and needed to be replaced. In accordance with the old landscape style adage, 'What is, is the great guide as to what ought to be', a well thought-out reconstruction plan was made. The plan reinforced the strengths of the original designs by J.D. Zocher, Jr. and C.E.A. Petzold and incorporated them in a modern design. Water gardens were connected, groups of trees were halved or replanted, visual axes were restored – right across the ring road! – and the car park will be relocated in the woods. No slavish clinging to the original layout of the park and later extensions but, instead, a unified vision of a twenty-first century country estate.

A recreational park as a work of art

The concept 'garden art' regained its true, original meaning in a park in Amsterdam, the Wilhelminapark near the Confectiecentrum [World Fashion Centre]. It was commissioned within the framework of the Dutch law requiring one percent of the cost of new public buildings to be spent on art, and was designed by Fortuyn/O'Brien. The park is enclosed on four sides by blocks of flats. Fortuyn's point of departure was that gardens are the pinnacle of luxury. Unlike buildings, gardens are non-productive in an economic sense; they are pure artificial art. Hence, visitors to the park are regarded as people viewing art, in this case an artificial outdoor space. Walkers in the fringes of the park are regarded as objects that may occasionally be seen as part of the plantings. People walking their dog or treating their noses to the fragrances of the garden, or the father of a child playing in the playground, they all have a walk-on part. On the large lawn in the middle, however, walkers have no role to play. Here they are on their own, unprotected, clearly visible from all windows looking out over the lawn. The park supervisor is as much a gallery manager as a gardener. Mowing the lawn is done in fanning-out circles, while some parts are not mown. In these places flowers blossom in spring, birds nest a little longer and rabbits play leapfrog in the morning sun. When finally the whole lawn has been mown, circles appear in various shades of green and yellow. The hay is dried in pushed-up ridges or is carefully arranged in fragrant piles. Then, one morning, all is raked away and a neat, empty field remains. The artist has consciously created a feeling of wide open space in the middle of the busy, compact city.

The Forestry Commission presents: entertainment

Belts of trees bordering clearings form an ideal background for sculptures, opera or drama. In the summer of 2001 so many outdoor cultural events were held that the newspaper NRC Handelsblad devoted a special column to sculpture gardens and open-air performances in its entertainment section. Nature outings could be combined with all kinds of large-scale events. Take your seat at a garden table and dine with two hundred other guests, or hand in your coupon and receive a picnic basket. Take a ferry or get into a canoe. Enter the woods (armed with a map) and scout the canopy above for a work of art in the shape of a horse cadaver. Do not forget to bring cushions, mosquito repellent and a raincoat. Even the Forestry Commission joined in the fun. In the city of Almere jet skis raced through the canals and disco music droned as the evening fell. After an evening show a long stream of visitors would leave the open-air theatre and walk to their cars or a shuttle bus, under a starlit sky along lanes without street lighting. Grease lights mark the way and some may tarry to read show-box poetry along the route, compliments of the Forestry Commission.

Everything is a garden, or is it?

In the nineties, the layout and design of parks and gardens in the Netherlands presented a typically eclectic, fin de siècle mixture. All kinds of styles were mixed or quoted, sometimes ironically. The scale of natural gardens was somewhat unnatural at times and then, some heartbreaking, old plantings would have to make room for new plantings. Architectural ideas and techniques were also applied to landscape and garden architecture. Green glass combines well with blue-green hydrangeas, producing shiny reflections all the year round. The 'green' experience was also combined with shapes borrowed from the visual arts and the building industry. This was not new in itself, but on this scale it was. There is an alarming side to this 'automation of green spaces'. Modern landscape architects have no horticultural background, let alone practical experience of ecological systems. Moreover, modern 'parks made to order' are not allowed time to develop. On the contrary, landscape architects' principle of 'manipulability' only concentrates on the architectural properties of gardens. In the Floriade show of 2002 there is only one pavilion that is there 'to stay'. Large, dominating, manageable trees and groups of trees, and hedges and lanes do receive plenty of attention. In contemporary garden architecture, also in reconstruction of historical gardens, the role of plants is marginal. Penelope Hobhouse, dean of English gardening culture, once complained that plants were not a topic on the agenda during a three-day congress on gardening history. Plant lovers and designers have retreated to their own separate garden compartments.

Landscaping in a wider perspective

In 1995 the foundation Perennial Perspectives was established in reaction to constructivist landscaping, which was more concerned with layout and trees than with plants. This international foundation propagated a new approach to landscaping and garden design. Dutch members of this international society include Piet Oudolf, a garden designer, Hein Koningen, promoter of natural habitat gardens, and Rob Leopold, a seed grower. In their view the various disciplines and schools should no longer regard each other as competitors or even incompatible, but as complementary. Horticulture, garden art and landscape architecture should allow themselves to be influenced by other disciplines to raise their art to a higher level. With this view, the group followed the ideas set forth by Jac. P. Thijsse in 1946. His ideas were put into practice in several natural habitat gardens and parks. The aim is to maintain a balance between plants and their environment. Perennial Perspectives organized a conference in 1996 titled 'Creative ecology and integral landscape design'. Subjects included the role of perennials in parks and gardens, natural habitat gardens, and garden photography. The broad range of topics and the diversity of the participants reflects the foundation's broad range of activities. Its aims include integration of ecology and landscape architecture, dissemination of horticultural knowledge and experience, and the creation of low-maintenance public and private parks and gardens. Evidently, members and followers need to be inquisitive, open-minded and flexible to be able to assess the inherent strengths of the various disciplines involved and to be able to toy with these in order to achieve good results. 'Form follows feelings.' Plants, nature and art must be the starting point for garden design. This principle may lead to surprising results: baroque cascades of plants, or a single, perfectly placed juniper. If the nature-loving ideas are pure, the results can only be good. Perennial Perspectives, also referred to as Dutch Gardening, or in German-speaking countries 'Holländische Welle', brought new, international inspiration on the brink of the new millennium.

Plant Shop Bulletin 1989

In the Moerheim plant shop, by 1989 the emphasis had shifted from plants to their environment. The year 1989 being the Year of the Butterfly, the catalogue features buddleia. A lime test day was held and the plant packages are still on offer. Special offer: forty perennials and a free planting plan. A new fragrant rose, 'Gina Lollobrigida', was introduced. The Daffodil Paper White can be grown indoors on hydro-grains. This month, the naturalization package offers bluebells (scilla non-scripta). Free tickets for Mien Ruys' gardens are available. Ten years later, towards the turn of the century, the nursery was closed. The town council of Dedemsvaart considered building a housing estate on the former seed-beds. The experimental gardens still exist, however, a living testimony to a glorious century of gardening at a famous nursery.

Moerheim Catalogue (1989)

158

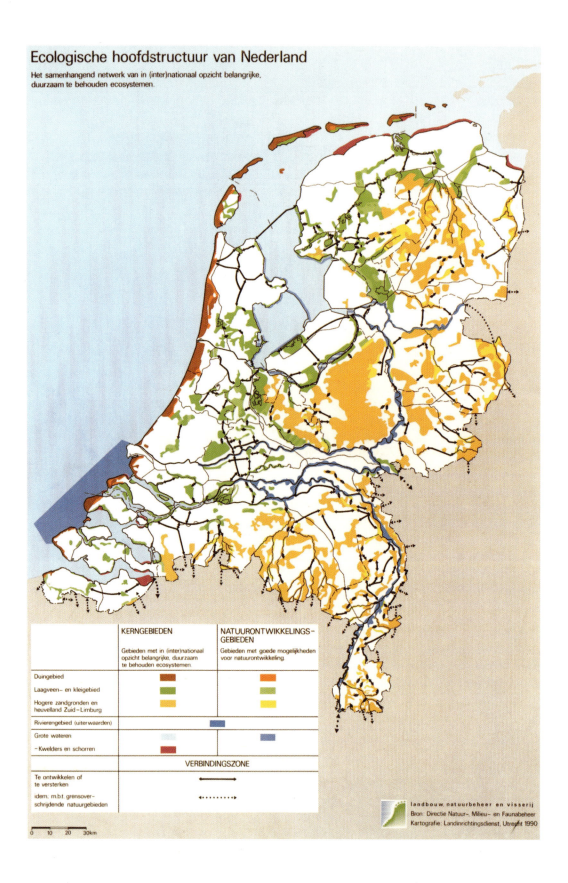

Ecologische hoofdstructuur van Nederland

Het samenhangend netwerk van in (inter)nationaal opzicht belangrijke,
duurzaam te behouden ecosystemen.

	KERNGEBIEDEN	NATUURONTWIKKELINGS-GEBIEDEN
	Gebieden met in (inter)nationaal opzicht belangrijke, duurzaam te behouden ecosystemen.	Gebieden met goede mogelijkheden voor natuurontwikkeling.
Duingebied		
Laagveen- en kleigebied		
Hogere zandgronden en heuvelland Zuid−Limburg		
Rivierengebied (uiterwaarden)		
Grote wateren		
− Kwelders en schorren		
	VERBINDINGSZONE	
Te ontwikkelen of te versterken		
idem; m.b.t. grensover-schrijdende natuurgebieden		

0   10   20   30km

landbouw, natuurbeheer en visserij
Bron: Directie Natuur-, Milieu- en Faunabeheer
Kartografie: Landinrichtingsdienst, Utrecht 1990

Main ecological structure in the Netherlands (1990)

Bureau B+B town planning and landscape architecture   garden no. 16 'Looking for Jane' in the Makeblijde

garden, Houten (2000)

Bureau B+B town planning and landscape architecture, J. van der Kloet   gardens at the Dutch pavilion Expo,

Hanover (2001)

J. Copijn country estate, Eelde

L. Baljon garden Rijksmuseum Twente, Enschede (1994)

M. van Gessel garden for canalside house Herengracht 72, Amsterdam (1998)

E. Proost garden at the Netherlands Design Institute, Amsterdam

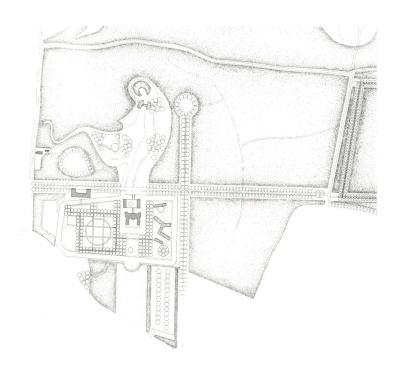

Bosch en Slabbers recovery plan Westhove - country estates Westhove, Berkenbosch and Duinbeek,
Oostkapelle (1995)

M. van Gessel plans for country estate Twickel, attempt to keep or bring back the best of every design period

West 8 landscape architects planting scheme Schiphol (1992)

Quadrat   Eva Cohen Hartogkade, Kop van Zuid, Rotterdam (1995)

Quadrat   Kadeslandtongplein, Pilot 24, Kop van Zuid, Rotterdam (1995)

West 8 landscape architects garden for Interpolis, Tilburg (1995)

W. Snelder   restoration gardens Château Neercanne, near Maastricht (1998)

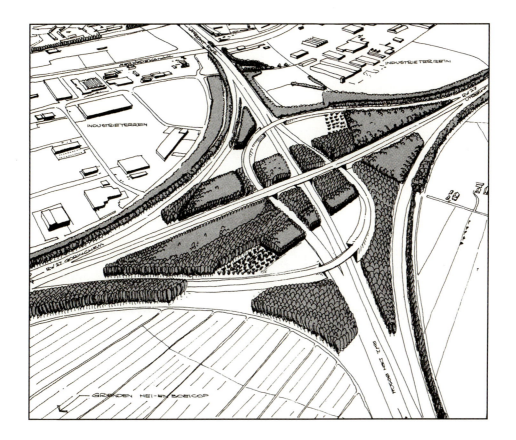

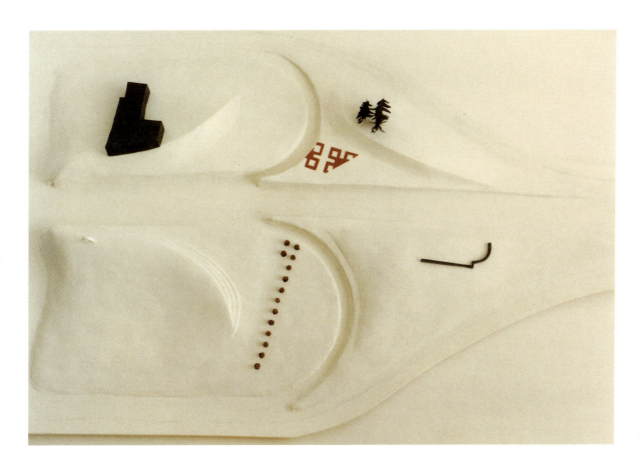

Forestry Commission road junction RW2/RW27, Vianen (1994)

A.M. Backer brings back a country estate between the slip roads to the A1 (1994)

S.I. Anderson Museumplein, Amsterdam (1990)

172

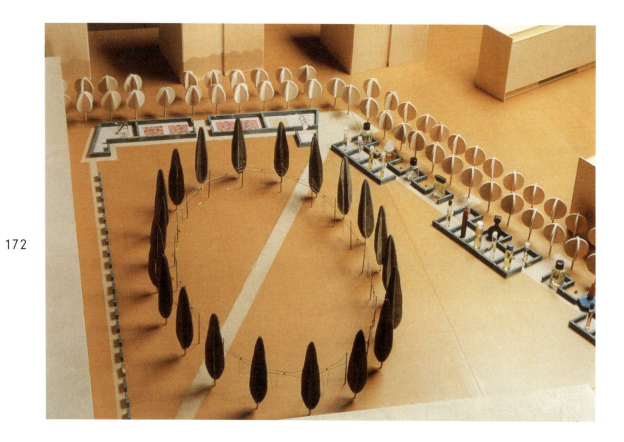

Fortuyn/O'Brien scale-model for the Wilhelminapark (1994)

Fortuyn/O'Brien turns the Wilhelminapark in Amsterdam-West into a continuous operation with the use of circles of light (1994)

N. Roozen   master plan Floriade 2002, Hoofddorp (2000)

Register

Photocredits

Colophon

The publication of this book was made possible
in part through the financial support of The Netherlands Architecture Fund.

Text Editing
  Hermine Hamhuis
Picture Editing
  Ingrid Oosterheerd
Translation
  Pierre Zeevaarder
  Michiel Zeevaarder
Design and lay out
  Lex Reitsma
  Leon Bloemendaal
Lithography
  Scan Studio, Heemstede
Printing
  Veenman drukkers, Ede
Production
  Paula Vaandrager
  Marianne Lahr
Publisher
  Simon Franke

NAi Publishers is an internationally orientated
publisher specialized in developing, producing
and distributing books on architecture, visual arts
and related disciplines.
www.naipublishers.nl info@naipublishers.nl

It was not possible to find all the copyright holders of the illustrations used. Interested parties
are requested to contact NAi Publishers, Maurits-
weg 23, 3012 JR Rotterdam, The Netherlands.

Available in North, South and Central America
through D.A.P./Distributed Art Publishers Inc, 155
Sixth Avenue 2nd Floor, New York, NY 10013-1507,
Tel 212 6271999, Fax 212 6279484.

Available in the United Kingdom and Ireland
through Art Data, 12 Bell Industrial Estate, 50
Cunnington Street, London W4 5HB, Tel 208
7471061, Fax 208 7422319.

Printed and bound in the Netherlands

ISBN 90-5662-243-9